American Reform Tract And Book Society

Aunt Sally

The Cross the Way to Freedom : A Narrative of the Slave-Life and Purchase

American Reform Tract And Book Society

Aunt Sally
The Cross the Way to Freedom : A Narrative of the Slave-Life and Purchase

ISBN/EAN: 9783744759151

Printed in Europe, USA, Canada, Australia, Japan

Cover: Foto ©ninafisch / pixelio.de

More available books at **www.hansebooks.com**

AUNT SALLY:

OR,

THE CROSS THE WAY OF FREEDOM.

A NARRATIVE OF THE SLAVE-LIFE AND PURCHASE
OF THE MOTHER OF REV. ISAAC
WILLIAMS, OF DETROIT,
MICHIGAN.

"Thou shalt no more be termed Forsaken, ... for the
Lord delighteth in thee."—ISAIAH lxii: 4.

CINCINNATI:
WESTERN TRACT AND BOOK SOCIETY.
1866.

PREFACE.

There are very few Anti-Slavery books adapted to the young, yet no field could furnish a more attractive literature for children than this. Robinson Crusoe and the Arabian Nights would seem lifeless and uninteresting by the side of hundreds of true and simple narratives which might be written of slave life in our Southern States. This story of "Aunt Sally" is, probably, no more remarkable than multitudes of others; only it has chanced to come to notice. It is strictly true in all its incidents. It has not been embellished, or wrought up for effect, but is given, as nearly as possible, in the words in which it was related to the writer. "Aunt Sally" is a veritable person, and is now living in Detroit, Michigan, with her son, Rev. Isaac Williams, who is pastor of a Methodist church there.

The portraits in this book have been engraved from daguerreotypes, which are faithful likenesses of "Aunt Sally," her son and his family.

The writer hopes that this little story may be the means of leading those who read it to think and feel deeply upon the truths which it involves, and that many more similar books may be written for our Sabbath Schools, so that the young may grow up imbued with the spirit of liberty, and rejoicing to labor for that oppressed and unhappy race which "Aunt Sally" represents, so, at length, this unfortunate people shall be slaves no longer, but shall find that, to them all, the Cross has been the Way of Freedom.

BROOKLYN, *N. Y., May*, 1858.

CONTENTS.

		PAGE
CHAP.	I.—Introductory	9
	II.—Introductory	16
	III.—Sunshine and Clouds of Childhood	24
	IV.—The Camp Meeting	33
	V.—The Wedding	46
	VI.—A Slave's Work and a Slave's Home	55
	VII.—A Husband Sold	66
	VIII.—A New Husband—Children Sold	78
	IX.—The Home Desolate—the Mother Sold too	88
	X.—The Slave-Pen	98
	XI.—The Slave-Gang	113
	XII.—Almost Despair	127
	XIII.—Sold Again—Gleams of Light	138
	XIV.—The Lash—Flight and Return	149
	XV.—The Tyrannical Mistress—A Slave's Sabbath	162
	XVI.—News from a long-lost Son	170
	XVII.—The Light of Hope at last	180
	XVIII.—Hope Realized	192
	XIX.—A Home in Freedom and Peace	207

AUNT SALLY.

AUNT SALLY.

CHAPTER I.

INTRODUCTORY.

Mother! it is the holiest word
That ever out of heaven was heard!
Her heart beats on, though free or slave,
All warm for those whose life she gave;
And sooner can the verdant cane
Forget its liquid sweets to gain,
And the magnolia's flowers of snow
To open when the soft winds blow,
And the lone stars to shine above,
Than I'll forget her faithful love!

Some twenty-five years ago, in Fayetteville, North Carolina, a slave boy, named Isaac Williams, was suddenly told that his mother had been sold to a speculator, and was going to Alabama. He loved her with all the ardor of a young heart which had nothing else to cling to, and when these terrible words fell on his ear, he sank down, overcome with anguish and dismay. All the past came back to him, sorrowful indeed, but endurable because shared with her. His earliest recollections were of those long days in the ricefields, when she carried him securely fastened to her back, with his baby brother tucked in her dress in front, because she would not leave them to be neglected in her cabin, nor lay them down, where snakes might crawl over them, by the side of the fence. How weary she must have been, his young mother; for then she was scarcely seventeen; but yet how kind she was; how patient when he was tired and fretful! He thought of the many evenings he had seen her spinning by the light-wood fire, that she might have yarn for knitting socks, wherewith to purchase a jacket or a hat or a pair of shoes for his Sunday wear, or sewing industriously to make or mend some needful garment, when so fatigued with the day's labor that she nodded between the stitches, and at last sat down in heavy slumber over her work. He thought of all the prayers she had offered for him, and of her faithful counsels as he came to maturer years. He remembered her grief when his father was sold from her, and yet the meekness with which she yielded to what she could not prevent, and the quiet cheerfulness and energy with which she toiled to provide a comfortable home for herself and her children when she had hired her time of her master. All these and a thousand recollections more flashed upon his mind as he heard of her fate, and ran to ask his master's permission to go and bid her farewell. It was granted, and first he went to the little house which she had rented, and where she had earned her living by the sale of cakes and beer. He opened the door. All was confusion. The few articles of furniture, which she had labored so hard to obtain, were either removed or lying in disorder about the room. The bright fire was out, the welcoming voice was silent. Upon inquiry, he learned that her purchaser had taken her, with many others, to a "wagon-yard," or, more properly, slave-pen, where they would be kept securely till he was ready to start on his distant journey. Thither he bent his steps. When he reached the place, he found that his old grandmother, who lived several miles farther in the country, had heard also of her daughter's sale, and had come with tears and tremblings to bid her adieu.

Can you imagine a scene like this? Can you think of your mother, who, dear as she is, is no dearer to you than Isaac's was to him, torn by brute force from her home, shut up in a narrow yard like a wild animal in a cage, her every look and tear watched by her purchaser, who walks about, whip in hand, to quell any who may be refractory, and her last agonized words of affection spoken to you through a crack in the fence which guards the enclosure? Yet all this the poor boy had to suffer, and his heart was as tender as yours.

What would you do? Would you become almost frantic in your grief, and rave wildly at the master, and strive to break down the bars and release your mother from so terrible a captivity? Would you? Then you would be guilty of treason and rebellion in the eyes of the law, and her owner would be justified in imprisoning you—nay, in taking your life if he deemed it expedient. Merciful Father! pity those whom no man pities, and by thine own power elevate those on whom the world and the world's law tramples!

So poor Isaac could only sob as if his heart would break, and wonder why he and she were ever born (was it strange?) and resolve with his whole soul, that if God spared his life, he would one day be free, and seek out his mother, and redeem her, though she were sold to a thousand Alabamas. Thus they parted.

The slave-train moved off, and Isaac and his old grandmother returned to their respective masters. How dark seemed the way to him now. He could no longer anticipate, as heretofore, a Sunday visit to his mother, and a treat of cakes and beer. There was no one to speak an affectionate or encouraging word to him. Sometimes he was tempted to be wholly discouraged, but he determined to rise above such a feeling, and to keep unchanged his faith in God and his purpose of freedom. So several years passed away, during which he grew to manhood, when a death occurred in his master's family which rendered a division of the property—that is, of the men and women—necessary, and Isaac fell to a relative in Mississippi. Farewell to North Carolina! True, he was still a slave, but he felt that in some way he was moving toward liberty, and so went gladly over the mountains and rivers to his untried home.

He had not been long settled there when, in 1833, he married a young colored woman, on an adjacent plantation. And now that he had a wife and children growing up about him, did he lose sight of his early resolution? By no means. He was always revolving in his mind how he should compass his own freedom and regain his mother. In 1838, his master went to Mobile, and Isaac accompanied him as his waiting-man. There was then living there a cousin of his mother's, an intelligent slave woman, named Mary Ann Williams. To her he applied, hoping she could give him some information. He was disappointed; she knew nothing of her cousin's fate, but promised to remember her, and as she could write, to communicate to him everything she might be able to learn. Meanwhile his wife's freedom was purchased by her father, and Isaac, hiring his time of his master, went to Orleans and worked as a carpenter until he had gained his own. But he did not forget his mother; she was always the burden of his thoughts and his prayers. How many plans did he make to ascertain where she was; how many letters did he write to Tuscaloosa and Mobile, and to every place where he thought there could be the least possibility of gaining the desired intelligence! At length, when he had almost despaired of success, he received a letter from Mary Ann Williams, at Mobile, telling him that, by a singular incident, which will be narrated hereafter, she had learned that his mother was living, and owned by a man, whose name she gave, in Dallas county, Alabama. She was alive then! She had not died on the fatiguing journey, nor been beaten to death by a cruel overseer, nor allowed herself to waste away with grief at her ruthless separation from all she loved. He thanked God, and wrote to her master, telling him of his purpose to redeem her, and asking him to name the price at which she would be sold. Long he waited for an answer; she was doubtless valuable to her owner, and he was unwilling to part with her. Again and again he wrote, but to be disappointed.

And now Isaac resolved to leave Mississippi. He wanted to breathe the free air. After various adventures, he at last reached the Northern States with his family, and finally settled in Detroit, Michigan.*

* The details of Mr. Williams's life are not given, as he intends eventually to publish his own memoirs.

CHAPTER II.

INTRODUCTORY.

It may gladden the diver's heart to gain,
    From the depths of the Indian sea,
A pearl as fair as the dew-drops are
    That lie on the summer lea.
And sweet to the hunter passing through
    The woodland's leafy door,
May come the song of a timid bird
    That never was heard before;
And the breath of a flower by the brooklet's side,
    That all unseen till then
Has opened its buds to the wooing airs
    Of the silent forest glen.
And blest it may be to the lover's thought,
    To win from the world so cold,
The bride with her warm and trustful heart,
    In his tender arms to fold.
But the love for her who gave me birth
    Is richer than ocean mines;
I would rather gaze on my mother's face
    Than the purest pearl that shines!
And list to her songs when day is done
    Than the notes of the rarest bird,—
More grateful than choicest flowers' perfume,
    Would be every soothing word.

And the lover's delight is weak and faint
   To the joy that would fill my breast,
If far from her sad and ceaseless toil,
   I could bear her away to rest.
Oh Thou, who dost pity the poor, look down,
   And grant to my life this glorious crown!

YEARS of anxiety and effort and hope deferred went by. At length, in 1852, Isaac received from his mother's master the long-desired letter, saying he would sell her to him for the sum of four hundred dollars. But now that the old trouble was over, a new fear tormented the faithful son. Was this woman *really his mother?* More than twenty years had passed since they were separated, and the only evidence he had of her existence was the testimony of her cousin in Mobile. Slight foundation it seemed upon which to rest so weighty a matter. Might it not be merely a plan of her master's to lure him into the dominions of slavery and punish him for his free spirit; or else to dispose probably of an old and useless servant? His heart sickened at the thought. He must be sure that he was right before he went further, for to be disappointed at last would be more than he could bear. So he wrote a letter to the master, asking him to put various questions to her, relative to incidents in his early life, with which she only was acquainted.

If your mother had been lost for twenty years, and you hoped to regain her through the remembrances of your childhood, how would you recall the birthday festival, and the prayers for you beside your little bed when your head was on her bosom, and the twilight walk through the rose-scented lanes when she told you a story of her girlish days, and that sad morning when, for an outbreak of passion, you fell into disgrace with your father, and she soothed and calmed you, and gently led you back to the path of duty and of love! Isaac was a poor slave boy when he knew a mother's care, but servitude can not crush out the heart's flowers, and he had remembrances which were sweet to him, and which he knew would wake a response in her heart if living she were. How anxiously did he wait for that letter which would be life or death to his hopes! It came at last. His questions were more than answered. Taking up the incidents as he narrated them, she had gone farther and recalled many things which he had forgotten, and sent them to him in her simple words with messages of affection.

That night what fervent thanksgiving did he send up to heaven for the blessed knowledge that he had a mother—he who had been so friendless in the world; that she loved and trusted him, and perhaps was even then supplicating their common Father for her distant son.

He now set about preparing to raise the money for her liberation. In March, 1856, he left Detroit, stopping wherever he had friends, or could make them, and finally reached New York in early autumn, having some two hundred and fifty dollars collected.

After a few weeks in the city and vicinity, he raised the balance of the amount, and then a new difficulty arose. How was the money to be transmitted, and his mother brought North? For experience has shown that it is a less troublesome and delicate thing to deal with Japan, and China, and Algiers, than with our Southern States, when it is desired to give to any of the colored population their birthright of freedom. Various plans were proposed and abandoned. At last he went to the office of Adams's Express Company, to see if it could be accomplished through their means. They declined doing it directly, but referred him to a well-known merchant of New York, as one who would advise and assist him, and for whom they would willingly undertake the matter. This gentleman listened to the story, and going to the Bank of the Republic, which is very popular at the South, deposited the money there, and arranged with the officers to have their correspondent in Selma, Alabama, purchase the woman and see her, with the requisite papers, consigned to the care of the Express company.

The burden of care was now taken from Isaac; the responsibility rested upon others. He had been buoyant and full of courage while active exertion remained, but when that was ended and nothing was left for him but patient waiting, the very intensity of his feelings gave birth to fears, and led him to count the chances for her safe release, and to brood over every possible disaster. She had been lost to him for a score of years, and he could have heard of her death at any time with comparative resignation, but now that she had come back to him in blessed resurrection, and the meeting seemed so near, her loss would be like shipwreck to the storm-tossed mariner, when just in sight of the green fields, and the peaceful spire, and the cottage of love for which his heart had yearned through all the dreary voyage. Disturbed and anxious, he went that evening to his lodgings, and retiring to rest, was soon lost in uneasy slumber.

And he dreamed. Some of his life-scenes passed before him like the moving pictures of a panorama, so real that the present was forgotten in the past they restored. He saw himself a boy, sitting on the dirt-floor of his mother's little cabin at Fayetteville, after a hard day's work, and pouring his sorrows into her sympathizing ear. He had just begun to realize what it is to be a slave. He had been accustomed to play with the master's children, and had had many little privileges about the house, but now that he was old enough to labor, he was kept in the field from dawn till dusk, under the eye of an overseer who had no leniency for his youth nor compassion for his fatigue. The poor mother could not point her boy to a brighter lot, so she only said, with a sigh, as she drew the "hoe-cake" from the ashes for their evening meal, "Well, Isaac, you must try and do your duty by mas'r, and the Lord Jesus 'll stand by ye. Near as I can find out, He had heaps o' trouble all His days."

The cabin faded away, and, almost a man in years and size, he stood by the "slave-pen," bidding her farewell before she went to Alabama. With unutterable grief he turned to depart, but her faith would not let her go without one word of comfort, so she called after him, "Keep a good heart, Isaac, and the Lord help ye! Put your trust in Him and He'll never leave nor forsake ye. Perhaps we shall see each other before we die!" This great anguish passed over, and he was in Louisiana, toiling for his freedom. Hundreds of dollars had been paid to his master, but obstacles were constantly thrown in his way, and he was sometimes on the point of rebellion and despair. But he thought of his mother, and seemed to hear her saying, as of old, "Be patient; keep on, and the good Lord 'll bring it all right one o' dese mornins." And then he was a free man in Detroit, and the pastor of a Methodist church; longing earnestly that his mother might share the advantages of his position, and feeling

AUNT SALLY.

inspired every day to labor by the remembrance of her christian virtues. And then he was in the actual present, and the money had been sent for her redemption, and he was trembling lest after all, the scheme might fail. In his dream he cried to heaven, "O merciful Father! shall all her faith and trust in Thee be for nought? Wilt thou not reward the love and service of sixty years?" And then he thought an angel bent over him and whispered, "Fear not, thy fidelity and hers have been chronicled. Wait a little while and thou shalt clasp thy mother in thine arms."

He awoke. The sun was shining brightly into the room, and having faith now that he was soon to meet her, he rose and prepared to leave New York for a little while, in order to raise the money necessary to defray their expenses till they should reach Detroit.

CHAPTER III.

SUNSHINE AND CLOUDS OF CHILDHOOD.

A CHILD should be a merry thing,
A butterfly upon the wing;
A bee upon a crimson clover,
With honey-dew half silvered over;
A crystal brook that 'neath the moon,
Glides onward through the nights of June;
A heart's-ease by a garden wall,
The loveliest of the lovely all;
A lark in heavenly circles singing,
Till the wide air with music's ringing;
A sunbeam dancing in and out,
Reflecting golden joy about;
Now sparkling like a rainbow braid,
Now lapsing when it likes to shade;
A soft and perfume-scented breeze,
Full of the tenderest harmonies;
Now showering roses from the tree,
Now opening roses yet to be.

Ah me! how few are born to this!
How few have felt love's sacred kiss
Upon their foreheads when they came
All radiant from the Eternal Flame!
The birds of song are cold and mute,
The honey-dew is gone for them,

Joy brings them but a broken lute,
And Life's tree but a flowerless stem.
Thank God! there is a brighter world,
Where every hope shall be unfurled
In sweet fruition to the air;
And all who yearn for love shall there
Upon the dear Redeemer's breast,
Find perfect love and perfect rest!

HAVING thus far followed the son, let us leave him among his Northern friends, and return to trace the history of the mother.

About the year 1796, (a slave's precise age is a matter of conjecture,) in a small cabin on a plantation not many miles from Fayetteville, North Carolina, a little colored girl was born. There were no great rejoicings when she came into the world. Her parents had been all their lives in servitude, and knew no higher pleasures than it afforded, but they felt, despite their ignorance, that their days passed wearily, and it was no joy to them to rear children for the same fate. No dainty wardrobe was ready for her use; no tiny caps nor embroidered dress, nor soft flannel blanket, but with her midnight earnings the mother had purchased two frocks of cheap print, to which her mistress had added one of her own children's cast-off dresses; and in this coarse apparel the little Sally, for so she was called, rolled about and stretched her chubby limbs as complacently as if she had been enveloped in a princess' lace and linen.

In a few weeks the mother returned to her labor in the field, and Sally was placed with old "Aunt Katy," who had charge of all the children on the plantation. At night, when the tasks were done, her mother took her to her own dwelling, returning her in the morning to the nurse. So she passed through babyhood, and grew into a stout little girl, running about the cabin and over the grounds, as unconscious of her relations to life as the dog with which she played, or the bird that sang in the old sycamore above the door. No pains were taken to develop anything but her animal nature—no one taught her to lisp the name of God, or to trace His hand in every object which surrounded her, or to regard His holy law in her daily life. Why should they? She was only a piece of property! Her mother, although possessed of more than ordinary intelligence and energy, was not then a religious woman. In spite of her hard labor, she managed to keep her cabin in better order, and her children more comfortably clad than most of the other servants; indeed, so full of life and spirit was she, that when the toilsome week was over, none enjoyed more highly the Saturday-evening dance or the Sunday holiday. She was a good mother, as far as she knew, and trained her children to habits of industry and activity. Speaking of those days, Aunt Sally said: "I tell you how my mother done me—she whipped me when I did n't work to please her, but 't was the gloriousest thing!"

The master required but little work of the child. It is policy to leave the slaves to grow and strengthen, unfatigued by labor, until they are old enough to be constantly occupied, as a colt is left unshackled, with free range of the pastures, until the "breaking" time comes. When about nine years old, Sally began to be employed in doing errands for her mistress, in sweeping the leaves from the walks, and in weeding the garden. She was full of fun and frolic, but she meant to be a good girl, and whenever she was blamed for any thing, although she tried to escape the threatened whipping, yet she was careful not to be guilty of the same offense again. There was a little girl, named Mary, about her own age who shared all her tasks. Rare play-fellows they were—talking and singing and running about together from morning till night. One bright day in Sally's tenth summer, Mary suddenly sickened and died. So full of life when the sun arose—so silent, so motionless, when it went down! It was the first bereavement Sally had ever known, and she was almost frantic in her grief. No one told her of death's brighter meaning; she saw only its sternness and gloom. Throwing herself beside the unconscious child, and sleeping only at momentary intervals, she consumed the night in calling upon her name, and when morning came, she went to the garden, and, gathering the choicest flowers, placed them in her hand, as if death were an ugly dream which daylight and bloom would scare away. So the weary hours went by, and when at evening preparations were made for the funeral, she begged to be allowed to join the procession. How strange and solemn it seemed as all the servants of the household, bearing lighted torches, walked two by two through the forest path to the burying-ground, preceded by the preacher, singing these dirge-like words—

"Bear her gently, calm and slow,
  To the home where she must go;
  One by one we'll follow on,
  By and by we'll all be gone
    Over Jordan.

"Deep within the pine tree's shade
  Has her quiet grave been made;
  Sleeping here and sleeping there,
  We shall meet from everywhere
    Over Jordan.

"Now we leave her to her rest;
  Jesus! Savior! ever blest,
  Take us soon from earth's alarms,
  Safe within Thy sheltering arms
    Over Jordan!"

The little coffin was lowered, the earth was thrown upon it, and with another wailing song the party returned. But Sally did not forget.

It was a balmy day in October. The fervid heats of summer were over, and there was a refreshing coolness in the air. The garden was gay with autumn flowers, and every waft of wind that went over the trees, bore to the ground the broad leaves of the sycamore to rest upon the myriad needles of the pine. In one of the paths stood Sally, broom in hand, busy in removing them as they fell. She looked up and saw, approaching, her young master, a handsome youth, elegantly attired, and having in his face and manner a certain reckless frankness which defied the judgment and straightway won the heart. Sally's quickness pleased him, and he often stopped to exchange a kind word with her.

"This wind keeps you busy, eh, Sally?"

"Yes, Mas'r. Don't more 'n get 'em swept away 'fore down they comes agin."

"Is that what makes you look so sober?"

"No. Mas'r. I's thinkin' 'bout Mary, an' wonderin whar she is, 'cause the preacher said, when they put her in the ground, she'd gone ober Jordan, an' we must all get religion an' follow on arter, an' 'pears like I dunno 'xactly what he meant."

"Now, Sally, don't you believe any such canting nonsense. When we die, that's the end of us; there's no hereafter. Look here," —and as he spoke he trod one of the yellow sycamore leaves into the earth—"see this leaf! In a few days it will be crumbled into dust; it's so with us when we die, and that is all."

"But, Mas'r, I thought mebbe we might

come up out of the ground sometime, like the flowers do in the spring."

"O, no, Sally, I tell you there's nothing after death. Don't bother yourself with such things," and he sauntered down the walk, and was soon out of sight under the arching trees. Just then a shower of leaves came pattering to the earth. Poor Sally sighed as she thought of their swift decay, and wondered if "young Mas'r," who was an oracle in her eyes, were right, and resolved that at least she would take his advice, and trouble herself no more about the matter.

She was now employed to carry every day to the field-hands their dinner. It was a long walk that she had to take across the pastures, with the bread and meat and boiled rice, borne in a large wooden bowl upon her head. A fence lay in her way, and one day, in climbing it, the bowl was upset and the provisions strewn upon the grass. In a tremor of fear she replaced them in the bowl and hastened on. Her delay was noticed, and the overseer coming up to her, whip in hand, demanded its cause. When he discovered some grains of sand sticking to the rice, she confessed the whole and begged him to forgive her. But forgiveness was not in his heart. He called her careless and lazy, and, seizing her by the shoulder, whipped her severely. She went home miserable indeed. She had nothing to turn to for comfort, and her future—

"It rambled out in endless aisles of mist,
The farther still the darker."

Every night she had to sit up late, carding rolls for her mother to spin, or spinning herself under her direction. Her only recreation was an occasional dance on Saturday evening. So in dreary monotony her days went on.

CHAPTER IV.

THE CAMP MEETING.

Out in the woods where the violet blows,
And the south wind opens the climbing rose;
Where the pale moss hangs from the lofty trees,
Banner-like, swaying with every breeze;
Where the fleet deer bounds at the break of day,
Light through the dewy paths away,
And the wild bird warbles his sweetest song
In the quiet of shadows when eves are long;—
There, afar from the noisy street,
Glad will I hasten my God to greet,—
And breeze and blossom, and bird and tree,
Gently shall speak of His love to me.

And then, when the pine trees sob and shiver,
And cast a gloom on the forest river,
I'll think of the errors that darken my years,
And pray for their pardon with bitter tears;
And when the sun through a vista beams,
And lightens the dimness with golden gleams,
My heart shall o'erflow in a song of praise
To Him who brightens the darkest days;
And prayer and song, where the boughs are riven,
Shall rise through the placid blue to Heaven!

COULD Sally banish from her mind all troublesome thoughts and reproaches of conscience because her young master had bid her do it? Ah no! Her heart was full of yearning and dissatisfaction.

When she was twelve years old she was a tall and comely girl, and went regularly to labor in the field. The only thing to which she looked forward with pleasure, was the dance at the close of the week; and her little earnings were parted with to procure now and then a bit of finery for this occasion. Sometimes she went to the Sunday prayer meeting, but was usually so fatigued that she slept through most of the services. If an alarming word fell upon her ear, and awakened uneasy thoughts, she tried to forget it, and to persuade herself that she had no cause for fear. But often, when returning exhausted from the field through the dim twilight, with the fading sunset glories before her, and the songs of happy birds in her ear, she would be so weary of the life she lived, and so full of vague longing for comfort and peace, that she would throw herself upon the ground in uncontrollable tears. Who was to help her? An ignorant girl on a lonely plantation, away from all exterior influences for good; obliged to toil from morning till night; surrounded by those as poor and simple as herself; with

the only educated and refined person who
ever noticed her, the only one to whom she
looked up as to a superior being, telling her
that there was "no hereafter;" that she had
only to work by day and sleep by night, till
at last she would drop into the ground and
crumble to dust like the autumn leaves. Ah!
there is One who never slumbers, and the
poorest and most neglected child is as dear
to Him as the loftiest king. He who feedeth
the young ravens when they cry, and without
whose notice not a sparrow falls to the ground,
was even then preparing her for rest and
joy through knowledge of Him.

September came, and with it a series of
camp meetings. There was great joy on the
plantation when it was announced that one
was to be held in the immediate vicinity of
Fayetteville. It was years since such a thing
had happened, and all the servants had the
promise of spending a day at least on the
camp-ground. As it was only two miles distant, it was easy for them to go and come,
according to the wish of the master. Sally
was wild with delight. She should see something of the great world, whose faint murmur
sometimes reached the plantation There

would be the handsome carriages which occasionally drove up to her mistress' door, and the fine ladies and gentlemen with their servants, from all the country round, and so many preachers, and such singing—it was bewildering to think of!

The important week came with cloudless skies. It was arranged that the servants should attend the meeting in turn, and Sally was not to go until the last day, Friday. Her excitement was in no degree lessened by the glowing accounts of those who preceded her. She could hardly wait for the time to arrive. Her calico dress was smoothed, a new ribbon was tied over her bonnet, and at five o'clock on Thursday afternoon she was ready to start with the others, in order to spend the night on the ground. How happy she was to have a week-time holiday, and to walk so blithe and free across the fields! Beneath this outward gladness, too, there was an undefined hope that she might obtain something to satisfy the craving of her nature. With snatches of hymns and merry words to her companions, she beguiled the way. An occasional tree obstructed the view, but at length she began to hear the faint hum of voices, and soon a quick turn in the path revealed the scene. A pleasant pine-grove had been chosen for the camp, and the white tents gleamed here and there through the dusky boughs. The horses and carriages were grouped upon the outskirts, and in the center many hundreds of men, women, and children were gathered round the preacher's stand, in the red light of the setting sun. A solemn hush was over the assembly, and as Sally drew nearer, the wind bore to her ear the words of the hymn with which the services were concluding:

"O! every weary, wounded soul,
  Come away;
'Tis Jesus waits to make you whole,
  Come away.

His precious blood was freely spilt
To cleanse you from your dreadful guilt;
He says, 'I'll save thee if thou wilt,
  Come away.

" The judgment day is stealing on,
  Come away;
Your hours of hope will soon be gone,
  Come away.

With Jesus do you wish to dwell,
And all his wondrous mercy tell,
Who saved your soul from burning hell?
  Come away."

The music and the somber pines brought back that other evening when she had seen her little playmate buried, and the tears rolled down her cheeks as she passed through the crowd and sought the tent belonging to her master.

The wind sighed all night through the trees, and the stars shone overhead. Sally lay down to sleep upon the straw floor, sorely puzzled to reconcile what she heard about the mysterious future. In her dreams, she thought her young master died, but came to her again in the garden-path, looking wan and wretched, and told her, in a voice like the wind in the pines, that he had been mistaken; that there *was* a hereafter, and that she must take warning by his miserable fate, and prepare to meet it. Then she thought she lay calmly on her own death-bed, and all who stood around rejoiced with her that her toilsome days were over, and that she was sinking into the sleep from which no master's call could rouse her, and from which she never could rise to pain.

The sun shone brightly into the tent, and she woke. The morning was glorious out there in the forest. The birds sang and the dew glistened, as they might have done in

Eden when the world was young. The early meal was soon despatched, and the tents put in order, for a new preacher was expected, and the closing exercises were eagerly anticipated by all. Carriages began to arrive, and by ten o'clock a vast congregation had assembled in the grove. Just in front of the platform sat Sally, in a seat which she had taken pains to secure an hour before. The people were becoming impatient, when a murmur was heard, and the expected preacher, who had ridden hastily from another meeting, passed through the crowd and gained the stand. He was a tall, slender man, with an impetuous manner, and a face which seemed to say:

"Be earnest, earnest, earnest;
Do what thou dost as if the stake were heaven,
And that thy last deed ere the judgment day."

He threw aside his traveling coat, and without delay began to sing, in a rich, minor voice, these words:

"Hark! 'tis the trump of judgment
That God's archangel blows!
O, sinner! will you hasten
To Jesus with your woes?

For on this little moment,
  Before the hour of doom,
Hang endless years of glory,
  Or endless years of gloom.

"Perhaps you do not hear it,
  Perhaps your heart is cold,
And earth's enticing pleasures
  Are all that you behold.
O, sinner! look and listen,
  And loud for mercy cry;
For in His sweet compassion
  The Savior passes by."

There was no heart that was not awed by the solemn music, and every head was bowed, as the preacher knelt to pray. Sally had never heard such a prayer. It was the outpouring of a heart that said—"I will not let thee go except thou bless me," me and all this waiting congregation. It was talking with God as friend talks with friend, till Sally believed in His existence with her whole soul, and expected to see Him appear in the parted sky, and answer with audible voice the strong petition. When it was ended, the preacher rose, and, opening the Bible, read the parable of the tares of the field, selecting for his text the closing verses:

"The Son of man shall send forth His angels, and they shall gather out of His kingdom all things that offend, and them which do iniquity, and shall cast them into a furnace of fire; there shall be wailing and gnashing of teeth."

"Then shall the righteous shine forth as the sun in the kingdom of their Father. Who hath ears to hear, let him hear."

There was no logical introduction, no display of doctrines, but the truth was sent straight home to every hearer as if he, and the speaker, and God alone were present. In simple words, and with imagery drawn from the scenes about them, the preacher portrayed their duty and their danger. "This morning," said he, "as I was riding through the forest, I saw a little bird trembling and fluttering in the snare of a serpent. It would speedily have been devoured had I not sprung from my horse and killed the monster. Ah! thought I, this is just the way the devil snares poor sinners. Those of you who are in high stations he charms with riches, and honors, and worldly ease; and to those who are poor, and have little to hope for in life, he whispers, 'You have no need to trouble yourselves about doing right; you must take what comfort you can now, and rely upon happiness hereafter;' or else, he tells you, 'You may do as you please, for death will end your existence.' No matter what he says, you are in his power, and he is luring you on to destruction, and unless you call to Christ to vanquish him with speedy blows, he will swallow you up in infinite ruin."

Sometimes he rose to a higher, wilder strain. "Did you ever think what it would be to be cast out for ever from God? If it were for a million of years, you could endure that; but *for ever!*—that is unbearable. What is hell? Why, it is a great burning desert, over which the lost wander without shelter, or cooling draught, or momentary repose, unable to be quiet because of the fires of rage and remorse that torment them from within. In the center of this desert there rises a mountain, and on it is a huge clock. Once in a thousand years it strikes one, and as the mournful sound vibrates through the burning air, the wretched souls shriek out in echo, Eternity just begun! Eternity just begun!"

Having, with rapid gesture and passionate utterance, pictured the condition of the sinner, **he began to speak in gentle tones of "the**

Lamb of God, who taketh away the sins of the world." And he sang:

> "Whose is that voice so kind and sweet,
> That seems my inmost heart to greet? —
> That whispers, 'sinner, come to me,
> And thou shalt rest and glory see'—
>   'Tis Jesus.
>
> "And can the Lord of glory mean
> That I upon his breast may lean?
> Will He, so great beyond compare,
> Help me my heavy load to bear?
>   Will Jesus?
>
> "He will; and when this life is o'er,
> And toil and burdens are no more,
> How gladly from the earth I'll rise
> To endless bliss in Paradise
>   With Jesus."

Sally had listened with her whole soul to the preacher, and now these tender words quite overpowered her. Was she not a sinner? Had she not a heavy load to bear? Did she not yearn for sympathy and rest? She looked up with streaming eyes and saw just before her her young master, who, out of idle curiosity, had come to the camp ground. In spite of his irreligion, he was momentarily affected by the scene.

"So you like this, Sally?"

"O mas'r! 'pears like it's what I's been wantin' dis long time."

"Well, well," he answered, as he turned away, "get it if you can."

There was a fervent prayer that none there assembled might be among the lost in the Great Day, and then with shouts, and sobs, and fervent ejaculations, the meeting broke up.

It was almost dark when the servants reached the plantation. In distress and uncertainty Sally lay down that night to sleep, and, for the first time in her life, tried to pray. So guilty did she feel herself, that she would not have dared to do it, if that gentle invitation had not rung in her ears—

"Sinner, come to me,
And thou shalt rest and glory see."

In dreams she lived over the excitements of the day. She was aroused in the morning by the call to labor, and, bewildered, hurried to her plowing in the field. She was not the only anxious one. Many of the servants were awakened, and the usual merriment was hushed. Silently she went her weary rounds. She wanted the Savior, but she knew not how to find Him. Would He accept one so poor as she? And if He would, was she willing to give up all her known sins and follies for His sake? She thought she was, but she was ignorant, and had no one to guide her. She was distracted with her emotions. Her brain seemed on fire. Noontime came, and she stopped her team by the side of the field. The earth seemed to spin around her, and losing her consciousness, she fell, as if lifeless, to the ground. Her companions gathered about her, and bore her to the nearest cabin, where she lay for two days moveless and insensible. On the third day this trance-like state passed away, and she revived and was herself again. And in her dream she believed herself in heaven, and she thought the Lord Jesus came to her with the most loving words, and told her to be His child, and follow his precepts, and He would be with her in every trial, and bring her at last to His "rest and glory." Then she arose and went cheerfully about her accustomed labor, feeling that she was no longer friendless and alone.

"So," said Aunt Sally, "dat's de way I come through in dis low ground o' sorrow."

CHAPTER V.

THE WEDDING.

The wind sang soft in the sycamore trees
   As tender and sweet a roundelay,
As if it had been some heaven-born breeze,
   That out of Eden had crept away.

And the stars looked down with mildest eyes,
   As if, like the wind so soft and low,
Their shining had been o'er Paradise,
   Which only the souls of the blessed know.

No wail rang out on the silent air,
   No groan from the earth beneath their feet,
But, all unconscious, the hapless pair
   Went forth, the future so dim to meet.

SALLY's real owner was a maiden lady who was deaf and dumb. She had nearly a hundred slaves, but as she could not bear the loneliness of the plantation, she hired them out principally to her brother, and spent her time in traveling from place to place. Sally's mother was now taken to be her waiting-maid, and accompanied her wherever she went. This was a great grief to Sally, for as long as her mother was there, there was always a degree of neatness and comfort and enjoyment even, in their poor cabin. What household is there out of which the careful, provident mother could be taken, and not leave need and desolation behind her? The mother! why the family happiness centers in her; and this poor slave woman, in her narrow sphere, was as important as any white mother who graces an elegant house, and counts her children as her jewels! Somewhat stern she was, rarely talking much with her children, but training them to the best of her ability in all industry and honesty. Every moment she could gain from labor, was spent in spinning, and knitting, and sewing to keep them decently clothed. Her husband worked on a plantation fourteen miles away. Once a month he came to see his family.

"We was allers glad to see father come," said Aunt Sally, "cause he brought us 'coons an' 'possums, an' we had meat to eat. I thought drefful hard o' mother for makin' me spin nights; but she did n't say nothin', —'peared like she kep' it all in her head. One day she says to me, 'Sally,' says she, 'you dunno whar you'll eat your last pound o' bread;' but I thought to be sure I know; I shall eat it down in the rice-field."

Now there was no motherly care, and the

children were scattered. Sally would have been quite inconsolable, had it not been for her new-found trust and hope in the Master above. She was very young; she was very ignorant; she had nothing to help her to understand the Gospel; but the Spirit was teaching her, and in her poverty and loneliness she was learning those great life lessons which, in one way or another, all must apprehend who would enter the Kingdom. When she was tempted to do wrong and to despair, she thought of her heavenly vision, and the Savior again stood near her, and she was comforted, and the temptation flew away. She was fond of singing, and readily catching the hymns which she heard, she lightened thus many a toilsome hour. This, which she learned from a visitor at "the house," was a great favorite in those days:

"Jesus once was poor and lonely,
  And a manger was His bed;
He, the radiant King of Glory,
  Had not where to lay his head.

"'Come,' He says, 'all ye that labor,
  And ye heavy laden, come;
I to every soul am Neighbor,
  I will give you welcome home.'

"'Days to me were dark and dreary,
Lighted only from within;
Listen, every heart that's weary,
I will take away your sin.'
"'Fear not; on this bosom tender
The disciple found repose;
If thy love to Me thou 'lt render,
I will banish all thy woes.'
"Lord! I'll worship and adore Thee,
Through my darkened earthly days;
And in heaven, at last, before Thee,
Sing in nobler notes Thy praise."

A change occurred in the family. The old master died, and the slaves were transferred to the rule of "young Mas'r Harry," who has before been mentioned. A wayward youth, he had grown into an intelligent and active, but worldly and violent man. Soon after his accession to power, he married a lively young lady, from one of the aristocratic families in the vicinity, and made her mistress of the plantation. Sally now went constantly to her work in the field, but the lady's quick eye observed her, and she soon singled her out from the rest as the one upon whom to call when she needed any extra service in the house. Sally liked the change, and strove to please her.

Among the servants who worked on a distant part of the plantation, was a young man named Abram Williams. Sally was now thirteen years old, and her mistress decided that she should be married, and that this young man should be her husband. Both were her property, therefore the only part they had to play was to acquiesce in the arrangement. It happened very well in this case, but the same power could have been employed, had they disliked each other. What think you of a system which gives such unlimited control, not only over the time and labor of men and women, but over their most sacred affections? Sally had never seen him, and knew nothing about the matter, till one day, when she was in the house, her mistress said—

"Well, Sally, you're thirteen years old, and I want you to be married. There's a young man over on the plantation who'll make you a good husband. He'll come here soon, and you'll see him," and then followed an enumeration of his good qualities.

"Laws, Missis!" was the only reply Sally could make. After that she missed no opportunity to speak of him to the simple-hearted girl, till Sally said, "'Pears like 1 loved him 'fore ever I saw him." True to her word, the mistress sent for him. They were pleased with each other, as she had predicted, and as there was no reason for delaying their union, it was agreed that they should be married as soon as the hurry of the planting time was over. He was a kind, good-hearted man, and Sally was happier than she had been for a long time, in feeling that she had some one to love who would love her.

One pleasant Saturday afternoon, a few weeks after this, was fixed upon for the wedding. Work was closed early, so that the servants might participate in the festivities. Sally's scanty wardrobe had been growing less in her careful mother's absence, and now she had no decent dress for the occasion. Her mistress produced from her own stores an old white muslin frock, and added to it a bright ribbon for her waist, and a gauze handkerchief to tie around her head. Abram was equally destitute, and his coarse field dress was exchanged for the time for some cast off clothes of his master's, which made him look, so Sally thought, quite like a gentleman. As a special mark of favor, the ceremony was to be performed in the house. The hour came, and with their bridemaid and groomsman they stood up before the colored Methodist preacher who was in waiting. He opened the Bible and read the account of the marriage at Cana. Sally had never heard it before, and the thought that Jesus had been present at an earthly wedding, impressed her, more than anything had ever done, with the importance of what she was about to do. No one had ever taught her the sacredness of the marriage tie. She had heard it jested about, and had seen it lightly broken, and so it was to her rather an incident of life than one of its solemnities. But now an awe crept over her; she felt as if God were there, and resolved, in heart, to do all in her power for her new-found friend. The reading was followed by a prayer, and then they were pronounced husband and wife. There was a momentary hush in the room. All seemed touched by the services save the master, who had condescended to grace them with his presence, and stood leaning in the door-way, with a satirical smile upon his face. What were to him the words, "whom God hath joined together let no man put asunder?" Did he not know that if for any reason he wished to raise a sum of money, he should separate them, and sell them, with as little feeling as he would a horse or a bushel of rice? No wonder he smiled and thought it folly! The mistress rose, and going up to the young couple, wished them much of happiness and prosperity. She was followed by all the servants in their turn, and when the congratulations were over, she led the way to the open air, where a table was set upon the lawn. It was ornamented with a handsome cake, which she herself had made, and adorned with flowers. Sally, as lady of the day, was made to sit down and pour coffee for the company. When the repast was ended, the lawn was quickly cleared for a dance, in which the mistress insisted that the newly married pair should take the lead. Sally had never danced since the camp-meeting, but they all insisted that she would not be properly married unless she did so, and she was forced to comply. "Dat was de last time I danced," said she, in relating it; "'pears like 't want right, noway."

It was a gay party, and as evening came on, Sally's light-heartedness returned, and she thought she had never been so happy in her life. Ah! could she have looked into the future, and seen what deepest griefs would come to her through her affections, what gloom would have o'ershadowed her marriage eve! The light wind in the trees would have changed to a mournful wail, and the stars that now seemed to smile, would have gazed down upon her with saddest eyes. And the birds singing good-night songs in the sycamores above her—the happy birds who could choose their mates and live lovingly all the summer through without one fear of separation, how would their notes have pierced her heart, could she but have looked forward!

But no "coming event cast its shadow before," and in a merry mood the party broke up, and the servants sought their cabins.

CHAPTER VI.

A SLAVE'S WORK AND A SLAVE'S HOME.

In her humble cot, the wife
Led a toilsome, happy life.
Busy, blithesome as a bee,
Not an idle hour had she.
When the day began to dawn,
Light and active as a fawn,
Up she sprang from slumber sweet,
The ascending sun to greet.
Hers the task, the pleasant care,
Simplest viands to prepare,
And the little ones to guide,
Nestling fondly at her side.
Sweet, when toilsome day was over,
'T was to see the husband-lover
From his labor home returning,
Find the cheerful hearth-fire burning;
And his wife, in comely dress,
Adding to her loveliness,
Waiting with the kindest smile
All his weariness to wile.
When the last "good-night" was said
O'er the children's cradle-bed,
How they talked, the happy pair,
Of the lot they loved to share!

Then, with prayer and heart-felt praise
To the God who crowned their days,
Laid them down to hours of slumber,
Such as angels love to number.

Pity not a home like this,
Lowly, yet so rich in bliss.
Pity those who ne'er can feel
They are one for woe or weal;
Who must toil from day to day,
'Neath a selfish master's sway;
And whose only joys arise
From the home beyond the skies!

The Sabbath morning rose clear out of the starry night, and with it came the necessity of Abram's return to his plantation, in order to be ready for Monday's work. Sally was distressed at this immediate separation. He was much older than herself, and her young heart was happy to have something to cling to, and to call its own. She prepared him the best breakfast in her power from the remnants of the wedding table, and then, tying a handkerchief over her head, set out to accompany him as far as she was able, on his homeward way. Hand in hand they walked through the dewy fields, trying to encourage each other with the hope that there would come a time when they should know no separation. The merry birds flew singing above them, the early flowers gave out their odor, the pines waved their branches in the breeze, clad in the fresh green of spring. Sally tried to restrain her tears, but when they reached the bounds of her master's plantation, beyond which she could not go without special permission, they burst forth anew.

"I know I's wicked, Abram, but I jest wish Mas'r Harry had to go 'way an' leave Missis like you leave me; I do! De white folks ken do jest as dey please, why can't we?"

"Don't cry, Sally," said kind-hearted Abram, "I'll come back an' see you soon as dey'll let me."

Sally had thrown herself down beneath the shadow of a pine, and sat for some minutes quietly. At length she exclaimed:

"I's wonderin' if de Lord knows how bad I feels dis mornin'. He had such heaps o' trouble, I specs He's sorry for us. Come an' kneel down, Abram, an' I'll pray to Him de bes' way I ken."

Together they knelt, and in simple, broken words she poured out her heart to Him who never slights the humblest cry. A strange peace filled her soul, and, rising, she bade her husband a calm farewell. He was awed by the prayer, for he knew much less of religion than she, and promising to see her on Monday night, if possible, he turned away, and was soon lost to the gaze amid the somber pines.

It was high noon when Sally reached home. As she walked up the long avenue that led to the house, the first object which attracted her attention was the carriage of her old mistress before the door. Then her mother had come —her mother, whom she had not seen for months! She ran quickly to the house to see if it were so, and was told by one of the servants that "Ole Missis" had really returned. She had been prevented from reaching home the night before by finding one of the bridges gone on the road to Fayetteville, and had arrived about an hour previous. To Sally's eager inquiries for her mother, she answered, that, after helping her tired mistress to bed, she had left the house. "I specs she's lookin' arter you, Sally; she took on powerful when she heard you'd done got married."

Sally hastened to her mother's old cabin, which now was hers, and, sure enough, there she was sitting on the low bed. She looked so neat in her trim waiting-maid's dress, that her daughter, who had approached unperceived, could not help stopping to regard her with admiration. A moment, and she was in her arms.

"Oh, mother, I's so glad you've come."

"Chile, chile," said the mother, while unwonted tears ran down her cheeks, "what have ye done? De Lord knows I'd rather have seen ye in yer grave than married. S'pose ye thought ye'd be better off, but chile, yer mistaken. Mebbe Abram Williams is a good man, an'll be kind to ye; but de kinder he is, an de more ye loves him, de worse ye'll feel by an' by. Do n't I know? Did n't I love your father better than all de world, an' wa'nt he allers kep' way on de big plantation, till now dey say he's sold to a speculator? An' den, when I laid out to take some comfort in my chil'n, an' worked so hard to take care of 'em, wan't dey all scattered an' carried off, de Lord knows whar, an' you only left in de ole cabin when I come home? Oh, Sally, gettin' married's de beginnin' o' sorrow; my heart aches to think what ye've got to bar! De white folks ken get married an' live happy all der days, but 'pears like dere's no peace for us no whar."

"Don't talk so, mother. Abram says he'll ask Mas'r to let him come an' live on de place, an' den we'll have good times."

"No, chile, it's no use. I knows. Dat's allers de way. Ole Missis goin' away to-morrow, an' I shall have to leave ye to suffer as I've done."

Poor mother! poor daughter! Silent they sat with their arms around each other, till the sycamore trees threw their evening shadows across the door. They had no plans to talk over, no hopes to impart; for what plans can they form who have no independent will? and what individual hopes can they cherish who exist solely for the benefit of others?

Sally's usual light-heartedness was not proof against her mother's despair. There was nothing in the past to which they cared to turn, and the anticipated future weighed them down with pain. At length, the gathering twilight warned the mother that her services would be required by her mistress, and she rose to go.

"Good night, chile; I must go now. Missis 'll want me, an' I shan't see ye again. Ye'll be gone to de field 'fore I ken come down here in de mornin'. *Do de bes' ye ken*, an' tell

Abram, yer mother says ye mus' be kind to each other while ye live togeder—de Lord knows how long dat'll be! Try to please young Mas'r an' Missis, so 's to put off de evil day—but it'll come, chile, it'll come, an' ye mus' be spectin' on't. 'Bove all, do n't forget yer prars, 'cause if de Lord aint yer friend, whar'll ye go?"

"Oh, mother, I's allers a prayin'—'pears like it's de greatest comfort I's got."

"Well, chile, dat's right. May de dear Lord bless ye! Far'well."

At daybreak the next morning, Sally was on her way to the rice-field. Her marriage had come and gone like any other incident in life, and now she must resume her daily toil. The hours went by slowly as she dropped the rice into the drills, and covered it lightly with her hoe. She had little disposition to talk with her companions, and had she desired it, it would not have been permitted. There was a new overseer on the plantation; a harsh, unfeeling man, who restricted the servants in every possible way. When the hot noon came on, they stopped to take their scanty dinner—a small piece of bread and meat, and some boiled rice. At a little distance was a spring of clear cold water, to which they had been accustomed to go to quench their thirst. But now even this was refused, because it occupied too much time, and their only drink was the water which ran along between the ridges of the rice-field. The mid-day meal over, in silence they returned to their monotonous tasks. Had they been free men and women, working for themselves and their children, with the stimulating hope of better fortune, which their labor should achieve, they would not have been monotonous; but when they could see nothing in the future but the same thankless toil, with the liability of losing, at any moment, the few domestic joys they possessed, it was weary work to scatter the grain and handle the hoe.

In the twilight, fatigued and hopeless, they sought their cabins. Abram did not come, as Sally had expected, and a week went by before she saw him again. "Now," said she, "I begun to see de hardes' times I ever see any whar in my life." With hard work, scanty food, a cruel overseer, an indifferent master, and a gay mistress, growing every day more careless and forgetful of her dependents, what chance had she for comfort?

A year of hardship passed away, and Sally's son Isaac was born. She loved him with a mother's tenderness, but not with a mother's joy; for, young as she was, she had seen so much of trial and privation that she could not regard life to one in her condition as a blessing. When she was able to return to her work, she could not bear to leave her baby behind her to be neglected, so she tied him into her dress, and carried him with her to the field. He was a sturdy little fellow, and grew apace, in spite of all his disadvantages. Once a month his father came to see him, giving what help and encouragement he could to the mother, and bringing her his little earnings, to assist her in providing for their child. Sorrowful meetings and partings they were, and yet pleasant, because all they knew of affection and sympathy was in them.

Two years more, during which nothing occurred to vary the dreary round of their existence, and another son was born, whom they called Daniel. It was the season of the year when all the fieldhands were engaged in plowing, and when he was three weeks old, Sally took her place with the rest. Now she had two children whom she would not leave behind, so one was placed securely in her bosom, and the other fastened to the skirt of her dress, which was rolled up in front to make a resting place for him. Thus burdened, she worked on, never losing her rounds, for a mother is a mother every where, in the rice fields of Carolina, or amid northern snows. It was not unusual for the women to take their children to the field, but they were accustomed to lay them down upon the grass by the fences. Sally would not do this, for upon a neighboring plantation a child so left had been strangled by a snake, and was found quite dead when the work was over. How many prayers did Sally send up to heaven in these dismal days! Were they not registered there?

The master grew daily more reckless and extravagant for himself, and more indifferent to the comfort of his slaves. "He fed us mos'ly on skim milk an' Irish potaters," said Aunt Sally, "an' peared like sometimes we should starve." On one of the adjoining plantations there was a kind and liberal master who gave his servants plenty of provisions. There is a strong community of feeling among the slaves, and they are always ready to assist those who are less fortunate than themselves. Sally knew that she should not appeal in vain to her neighbors, so many a night after all the household were in bed, she would take the horse which she used in plowing, and ride stealthily over to their hospitable cabins, sure always to get some dried meat, or a bag of meal, from the generous occupants. Then hastening back, in silence and watchfulness, she would cook a little for herself and her children. In ways like this she eked out their scanty fare, always anxious, and fearful of being discovered.

During this miserable time another child was born to her, but its little life was soon closed; and at evening, after working hours were over, it was buried in a rough box out among the pines. Sally did not mourn for it; she was glad it had escaped the misery of their earthly lot. No stone marked its grave, but the mother knew the spot, and sometimes stole out there at night to pray. She was always comforted, for God seemed near to her there, and she fancied the wind in the trees above her was singing her child's lullaby, and hushing it to sweet repose.

CHAPTER VII.

A HUSBAND SOLD.

See! the moon is over the hill;
Hark! the wind in the trees is still;
Only the stars shine out on high,
In the azure depths of the midnight sky.
The master sleeps in his downy bed,
And watch and care for a while have fled,
Wake, my children! and we'll away,
Ere in the east is the dawn of day.
Whither? Alas! I know not whither
This side of the cold and fatal River!
The earth has many a pleasant dell
Where ye and I might be sheltered well,
But ne'er secure on the land or sea
Can the slave from his white pursuers be!
God of mercy, and truth, and right,
Guide our steps through the silent night!

The master grew every day more reckless in his expenditures, and more unreasonable in his demands upon his servants. Among the household duties which Sally occasionally performed, was that of seeing that the milk was properly strained and taken care of. One morning her mistress was out of humor, and imagining that Sally had not taken pains with her work, she complained to her husband.

"Look here, Sally," said he, "do you put the milk in a pan that is n't washed?"

"Oh, no, mas'r, I takes partikler pains to have it clean."

"Do you mean to contradict your mistress?"

"I did n't, mas'r."

"You did n't, did you? I'll see!"

Seizing her by the arm, he whipped her severely, and at length desisting from very weariness, he called out, "Now see if you 'll tell the truth the next time."

Half crazed with pain and terror, she crept away to the field. She dared not neglect her tasks, and all through that wretched day she followed the plow, smarting from the blows. It was the crisis of her fate. Year after year she had suffered on, and now she felt that she could endure no longer. With her buoyant nature, she would not have despaired could she have seen one distant gleam of hope, but matters were daily getting worse on the plantation, and she knew not where to turn for light.

Revolving these things in her mind as she went her weary rounds, she came to the desperate resolution of running away, and with uplifted heart, she asked God to pardon her if she was wrong, and to help her if she was right. Communicating to no one her intention, she sought her cabin at the usual hour, and procuring her children's supper, eating none herself, so oppressed was she by her pain, and by the thought of what she was about to do. She dared not leave the grounds till all was quiet, and while the children slept upon the floor, she busied herself in collecting their little clothing, and tying it up in a bundle, which she could conveniently carry. The early moon was shining in the sky, and she must wait till it went down. As she sat there in silence, she wondered if she were about to commit a sin, for she had been trained to such implicit obedience to her master, that she hardly dared think of resisting his will. Suddenly she heard the sound of horses' hoofs, and of voices, coming up the walk. She remembered that her master had ridden over to Fayetteville in the morning, and it was his voice, and that of the overseer, to which she listened.

"Here's that girl, Sally, Mr. Green, you must look after her a little. She's never been fairly broken in yet. I made a beginning, this morning. You must train her."

"Ah! leave me alone for that, sir. I'll fetch her up to the mark. I'll give her a bigger task to-morrow, and if she do n't do it, she'll see what she'll get."

"The fact is, Mr. Green, I do n't care how much you get out of 'em. Things are going to ruin, and I must make more money in some way."

The voices died away, and with them Sally's irresolution. She would go at all risks. The moon went down, and all was still. Taking the sleeping Daniel in her arms, she gently shook the older boy, saying, "Isaac, Isaac, wake up chile. Do n't you want to go an' see yer father?" He opened his eyes at the words, and accustomed to obey his mother in all things, took her hand as she passed out—out into the night so pure and calm, with the holy stars above her, and the dewy earth beneath her feet. Abram was then at work on a plantation a few miles away, and thither she directed her steps. Avoiding the roads lest she should be discovered by some belated traveler, she hurried on through the fields, keeping, where it was possible, under the deep shadow of trees and fences. Now and then the cattle stirring in the pastures, or the neigh of a horse startled by her footsteps, would make her heart beat quick, and she would stop to listen; but no harm came to her, and carrying one, and sometimes both, of the children, and hushing their questioning cries, she at length reached her destination. Going softly up to the door of Abram's cabin, she entered and roused him from his heavy slumber. He was terrified to see her there with her children, but soon understood wherefore she had come.

"There's no time to lose, Abram. I heerd that Aunt Marthy was a-takin' in washin' in Fayetteville, an' I know she'll let me an' de chil'n stay with her."

Breaking in two a piece of hoe-cake which she had saved from her supper, she gave it to the boys, and rising from the low bed where she had seated herself for a moment, she took Daniel again in her arms, saying to her husband, "You mus' tote Isaac, Abram, he's done tired out, poor chile."

It was past midnight. Fayetteville was four miles distant, and Abram must return for his morning's work, so they hurried on. He knew the road, and as it passed through a quiet neighborhood, he was not afraid to keep it. They talked little, for fear of being in some way overheard, but arranged that Sally and the boys should keep hid for a while with "Aunt Marthy," and that Abram should see them as often as possible. Sally knew not what was before her, but in spite of the haste and the danger, it was delightful to be walking so far from the plantation and away from the overseer's eye. Stiff and sore from the whipping she had received, her heart was yet lighter than it had been for many a day. The dawn had not yet begun to glimmer in the east when they reached the town and sought the narrow street and humble cottage of "Aunt Marthy." A good old creature she was; owned by a man in Fayetteville, but hiring her time and supporting herself and her children by washing. She received Sally with open arms, without manifesting much surprise at her appearance. She had had the experience of many years, and she knew too well the chances and changes in the life of a slave to be astonished by them. "Laws, chile, I's been through it all, an' I knows ye can't bear it unless ye loves de Lord."

While it was yet dark Abram bid them good-bye and hastened away. It was now October, and from this time until New Year's, she lived quietly with Marthy, assisting her daily toil. The boys were so young that they would hardly be recognized, so they played about the street with the other children, but Sally never went out except at night; and then cautiously, and for short distances. During this time Abram was sold on to a plantation near Fayetteville, and he often stole in at evening to see his wife. He took pains to hear about her master, and learned from one of the servants that he was fearfully angry when he found Sally had gone, and threatened to kill her if he ever saw her again; also, that his slaves were not to work at home any more, but were all to be hired out at New Year's. Sally knew she could not long remain undetected where she was, and believing that her master would not touch her on account of his own interest, she resolved to go boldly when the day came and hire herself out with the rest.

The important morning arrived, and Sally

took her children and went out to a field on the old plantation where she had heard the business of the day would be transacted. What fervent prayers did her heart send up as she walked along! She believed they were heard, and her step was firmer and her courage stronger as she reached the ground. Her old companions were already assembled there, and a crowd of the neighboring planters were standing about, talking of the price and capacity of those they wished to secure. Among them was her master. He saw her, and muttering something between his teeth, appeared as if he would confront her as she advanced, but the gentleman with whom he was speaking, said something in a dissuasive voice, and he turned away. Sally's heart was full of thanksgiving as she took her place with the rest. She believed the Lord was with her as he was with Daniel in the lion's den. The sales went on, and her turn at last arriving, she was hired by a citizen of Fayetteville, an easy, compassionate man, who had heard of the unjust treatment she had received. A new hope dawned upon her. Perhaps he would let her hire her time as her aunt did. **She ventured to propose it to him, and he** agreed that for six dollars a month, regularly paid to him, she should be her own mistress, and do what she pleased. The moment that she was free to act for herself, with what spirit and energy did she take hold of life. She had always had a natural fondness and aptitude for cooking, and now she resolved to rent a small house, and commence the sale of cakes and beer of her own baking and brewing. Before a week had passed she had rented a little tenement of two rooms, and having procured a barrel of flour and other necessaries in advance, she was ready to sell to any one who would patronize her humble store. Her children were both with her at first. When she had time, she took in washing, and then she accustomed them to help her to beat the clothes. In a month she had not only paid for the flour, but she had also given to her new master the first installment of hire-money. Very judiciously she made her small purchases. She would watch the market-wagons as they came in from the country, and often buy her provisions to great advantage. Every morning she carried a gallon of hot coffee to the market for sale. The gentlemen soon learned to know her, and would buy a cup, sometimes throwing her fifty cents in return. She had never dreamed of having so much money as she now earned. She bought comfortable clothes for herself and her children, and obtained, from time to time, little articles of furniture for her house. And when, at the end of the year the same arrangement was made with her master for a much longer time, her heart overflowed with gratitude to God, and she resolved more and more to dedicate herself to Him. What was it that made her so happy? The privilege of working every moment for the support of herself and her children, and of paying out of her earnings six dollars every month to her master? Verily happiness is not absolute, but relative, in this world.

Abram still worked in the vicinity, and often came to see her and the children. He was a kind and affectionate man, but he had not Sally's strength of character and firmness of principle, and he was easily led astray. He had lately fallen into a habit of gambling, at which she was exceedingly distressed and alarmed. She knew from young "Mas'r Harry," the ruin to which it led, and while she begged him to abandon it, she loved him so well that she would sometimes give him money when he came and told her of his losses. At length his master discovered his visits to the gambling-room. He was not grieved at his sin, but angry at his disobedience; and, going to Sally, in a dreadful rage, he told her that, if her husband ever gambled again, he would put him into jail, and he never should come out from there as his servant. This frightened Abram, and for a year he kept away. But one night the old temptation returned again, and he went. His master heard of it, and threw him into jail the following day, as he had threatened. Sending for Sally, he told her what he had done, and that he should sell him to New Orleans.

"Oh, Mas'r, de Lord bless ye, won't ye try him once more? He was allers such a good man, an' so kind to me an' the chil'n!"

"Now, Sally, you may just stop your crying around here, for as sure as there's a God in heaven, he never shall come out mine."

There was no hope, then. He must be sold, and selling to New Orleans was to her like death. How many whom she had known had gone the same way and never been heard of

AUNT SALLY. 77

more! She would rather have seen him in his coffin.

It was late when she reached home, too late to go to the jail, and the night must wear away in prayers and tears. She was up with the dawn, and baking some fresh biscuit, and making a pot of her nicest coffee, she took them to the jail, and sat down upon the stone steps until the doors should be opened. Her mother's words came to her mind, and she wept bitterly. Her "evil day" had indeed come. The passers by looked coldly upon her. It was a common thing to see poor slave-women sitting, in tears, upon the steps of the jail. At length she was admitted. Abram was quite overcome, when he saw her, with remorse for his fault and grief at their separation. For they had loved each other, even as people do whose faces are fair! Sally strove with her stronger heart to sustain him and to lift his thoughts to God. But sorrow would have its way, and from nine o'clock till one, they sat weeping and holding each other's hands, as if it were indeed the death hour. At length the rude voice of the jailer was heard ordering her away. They clasped each other convulsively for a moment, but the husband could not speak. Amid her sobs, Sally exclaimed,

"Oh, Abram, far'well! Remember de Lord! Remember de Lord! I shall pray for ye, ye poor soul! Far'well, far'well!"

CHAPTER VIII.

A NEW HUSBAND—CHILDREN SOLD.

On the brink of a flowery meadow,
   A lamb by its mother lay,
All in the golden sunshine
   Sleeping the noon away.

The mother watches her darling,
   And opens her half-shut eye,
When over the flowery meadow
   The wind goes whispering by.

What moves in the trees behind them?
   'T is a wolf, all gaunt and grim!
He longs to tear in his hungry jaws
   The lamb from limb to limb.

One spring, and his prey he seizes,
   And into the wood so cold,
With savage delight he bears it
   Away from the shepherd's fold.

And the mother may watch by the forest
Till the meadow is white with snow,
But never from out its shadow
Her darling again will go!

"Oh," said Aunt Sally, "dat was de dreffulest hour I ever see in my life, when I turned my back on de jail. 'Peared like dere want nothin lef' in de world, an' when I tried to pray, dere want no God to hear me. I did n't mind my work dat day, but jest lay on de bed, cryin' an' groanin' as if my heart would break, an' wishin' we was all dead an' out o' trouble. De chil'n, poor things, tried to comfort me, but I thought, to be sure, dere's no comfort for me when dey sold my husband!

"By-an'-by, when it was dark, Aunt Marthy cum to see me. She heerd dat Abram was sold, an' she know'd well enough how bad I'd feel. Wal, she sot down on de bed, an' ses she, 'Sally, I's cum to pray wid ye, 'cause I know it's de only thing dat'll do ye any good.' I thought to myself, dere's no use a prayin'. Did n't I beg de Lord to let my husband stay, an' want he sold all de same as if I had n't asked him? But I did'nt speak, an' so she knelt down an' begun. At first I did'nt pay no 'tention to what she said, but she kep' on, an 'peared as like Lord Jesus was right in de room, an' she was talkin' to Him. She told Him how 'flicted I was, an' how I was almos' discouraged, an' begged Him to stan' by me, an' to be better to me dan de best husband in de world. All at once I thought p'r'aps dis was de cross I'd got to carry for Jesus, an' den 'peared like a great burden rolled off my heart, an' I could see my way clear through to heaven. Instead o' grievin', I wanted to praise de Lord for His mercy. Dere want no trouble any more; only de Lord, de Lord everywhar. When she'd done prayin' I got up an' begun to sing dis hymn. I'd often sung it afore in de meetins, but I never know'd what it meant till den:

> "'If there's a heavy cross to bear,
>   Oh, Jesus! Master! show me where!
>   And all for tender love of Thee,
>   I'll bear it till it makes me free.
>
> "'Free from the faults I long have known;
>   Free from the sins I dare not own;
>   Free from each care the world has given,
>   To keep my soul from Thee and heaven.
>
> "'And when I reach that glorious place,
>   And gaze with rapture on Thy face,
>   Dear Jesus! every cross shall be
>   A crown of joy for Thee and me!"

The next morning Sally resumed her usual duties, and was to be seen in market and at home attending to her customers. The ecstacy of the evening was gone, but something of "the peace of God, which passeth all understanding," remained. She could not think of her husband without tears, and for six months her health suffered from the shock she had received, yet Jesus seemed nearer to her than ever before, and she was consoled by the thought that He was a friend on whom she could rely, at morning and noon and evening. That sale was truly like death, for she never saw or heard from Abram again. When Isaac was twelve years old, he would have been taken from her and put to service, but he was such a comfort to her, and daily grew so helpful, that she could not bear to part with him, so for two dollars a month she hired him for two years of his master. Her kind Fayetteville master was pleased with him, because he was so bright and active, and offered to teach him to read if his mother would purchase the necessary books. This she gladly did, and as he learned rapidly, (albeit there was no white blood in his veins,) she soon had the delight of hearing the Bible read by her son. It was the highest pleasure she had ever known, to sit down with him in her neat little room, when the work of the day was over, and hear some chapter from the life of Christ, or some thrilling Old Testament story. One night, when he had been reading to her, slowly and carefully, for half an hour, she suddenly exclaimed,

"Laws, Isaac, I never 'spected to see de like o' dis—to hear you readin de Bible like de white folks. 'Pears like de Lord's been so good to ye, I hopes ye'll do all ye ken to serve Him."

"I's been thinkin' o' dat dis long time, mother; I b'lieve de Lord's got something for me to do."

"Yes, chile, we's all got something to do, an' we must be willin' to do whatever de Lord gives us. I's laid awake many a night, thinkin o' dis yer thing, an' prayin' de Lord to help me. When yer father was sold, I thought der want nothin' more for me, but de Lord He brought me through, an' I's made up my mind, 'taint no use calculatin' what He'll do. We mus' try to do right whar he puts us, an' den, if we's prepared for a better place, he'll show it to us. I specs ye'll be a poor slave all yer days, Isaac, but if de blessed Jesus is yer master, an' ye bar de cross for his sake, He'll make ye free at last in de Kingdom!"

The tears stood in the boy's eyes as he listened to his mother's words, and he resolved in his heart to do the best he could in life, and to trust the Lord for all.

When Abram had been gone four years, Sally's master began to look for another husband to fill his place. Sally had seen marriages so lightly made and broken, that it was to her a matter of course. Her respectability and thrift had procured her many admirers, and as her master deigned to consult her on the subject, she chose from among them a free colored man named Beggs, because she thought he could never be sold away from her. He bore a very good character, excepting that he was somewhat addicted to intemperance, but he rarely became intoxicated, or treated her with anything but kindness. He worked at his trade in town, and Sally continued her sale of cakes and beer. She did not love him as she had done her first husband, yet they lived quietly together, and, on the whole, happily. Isaac and Daniel were now away with separate masters, and Sally would have missed them exceedingly had not their places been partly supplied by the birth of a little boy, whom she called Lewis. Other children she had who died in their infancy, so that this little fellow, who was sprightly and affectionate, was doubly dear to her. She was now living in comparative ease and independence. Little by little she had added necessary articles of furniture to her house, and of dress to her wardrobe. Her two rooms, with the porch adjoining, were always neat and in order. Her baking and washing were dispatched in the morning, and then, with clean apron, and nicely folded handkerchief about her head, she was ready to attend to her customers, or to do any little job of sewing which she had taken in, for to her knowledge of cooking and housework she added no small skill as a dressmaker. She was able now to hire a girl to help her in the house, and when it became known how good a seamstress she was, she had much work brought her by the ladies in the vicinity. In her prosperity Sally did not forget the Lord. Most fervently did she thank Him every day for His mercy. Naturally hopeful and buoyant, she enjoyed the happy present, without daring or wishing to anticipate the future. She went regularly to church on the Sabbath, persuading her husband, when he could, to accompany her; and when Isaac and Daniel were permitted to visit her and to go with her also to the meeting, her heart overflowed with thankfulness to God. Sometimes they were allowed to go home with her to spend the Sabbath evening. This was indeed delightful. They must all go into the best room, which was her pride, with its high feather bed, covered with a bright patchwork quilt, its rocking-chair, its little table by the window, with the glass hanging above it, and its chest of drawers, which contained all the best articles of the family attire. Then she would bring out a plate of her choicest cakes, and treat them each to a cup of coffee, or a mug of her own innocent beer. These joyful evenings were always concluded by Isaac's reading a chapter in the Bible, and his mother's offering up a grateful prayer.

It would be pleasant to pause over this happy time in Sally's life; this little gleam of sunshine in her stormy sky, but events hurried on, and our narrative must follow.

Sally's old mistress on the plantation had been gradually declining in health for years, and now news came that she was dead. Her slaves were divided between her brothers and their children, and Sally and her sons fell to one of the nephews, a dissipated young man, who had wasted all his property, and had been waiting impatiently for his old aunt's death, that he might receive his portion of her estate. He wanted to convert some of his share into ready money, so Isaac and Daniel and Lewis were taken and sold in Fayetteville at a public auction. Daniel was bought by a planter far up the country; Isaac, by a gentleman who lived a little way out of the town; and Lewis, poor little Lewis, his mother's darling, with his merry face and sportive ways,—a speculator from Alabama, saw him, and purchased him to go with a "lot" he had in waiting, to that seemingly distant and unknown land. Sally's grief was great at parting from Daniel, whom she might never see again, for, although not so intelligent as her older son, he had always been affectionate and obedient to her. She took leave of Isaac with more hope, for he was not to be so far removed; but when it came to

Lewis, who was immediately placed in his purchaser's traveling wagon, she was broken down with anguish. The curse of servitude was upon her, although she had married a free man. She was still a slave, and her children were slaves, and only death could free them. Her distress was increased by the rage and despair of her husband, for he was as fond a father as she was a mother. She saw the money paid down for her boy; she heard him calling good-by to her out of the cart, and, half frantic, she ran to him, and catching him in her arms, held him tightly, as if they could never be parted. He was only three years old, just learning to talk, and every hour developing some new charm in his mother's eyes. He did not understand her grief, and she would not sadden his little heart by telling him he would never see her more. Pleased at the prospect of a ride in a wagon, he laughed and danced about, unconscious of fear or sorrow. Sally gave him a little ginger-cake, saying, as she put it into his hand, "Now, Lewis, break it in two, an' give mammy a piece."

"No," said he, "didn't ye jes' gin it to me?" The poor mother burst into tears, and the child, thinking it was all because she wanted the cake, exclaimed, "Here, mammy, I *will* gin ye a piece," and then her husband came and took her away. With streaming eyes she watched the wagon till it disappeared, and then, as she turned homeward, if she had been familiar with the Scriptures, she would have cried out in anguish, "All Thy waves and Thy billows are gone over me."

CHAPTER IX.

THE HOME DESOLATE—THE MOTHER SOLD TOO.

The house is desolate and lone,
My precious boy, now thou art gone.
I look upon thy empty bed,
And every joy from me hast fled;
I watch to hear thee on the stair,
But all is still—thou art not there;
And then my heavy heart sinks down,
And sees the cross, but not the crown.

I should be glad, my boy, to die
Beneath this Carolina sky;
Yet oft I fear my fate will be
O'er hill and plain to follow thee.
God help me! help us every one,
Through the dear love of Christ his Son!

IT was almost dark when Sally reached her own door. Her husband had left her on the way, and gone into a low drinking saloon, to drown his grief and anger in intoxication. Some of her neighbors and acquaintances were waiting for her return, and, going into the house with her, tried to cheer her heart. But what can comfort a mother when she is bereft of her children? If your three only boys should be stolen from you in one day, without hope of recovery, could any earthly friend console you? Sally's sons were as much to her as yours are to you, and the words of her visitors fell unheeded upon her ear. At length, seeing that their efforts were of no avail, they went out silently, and she was left alone. Alone! Yes, it was such loneliness as only they can understand, who have had a similar trial. For a while, she sat immovable, and, as if stupefied by her grief, and then she arose, and opening her little bureau, began to look over the clothes that had belonged to Lewis; every article of which she had labored hard to procure, and had fitted and made for him with a mother's pride and pleasure. The little frocks and aprons were taken up and laid aside again, but when she came to the tiny cap, with the jaunty tassel upon one side, in which he had looked so smart the Sunday before, and saw lying beneath it Isaac's precious Bible, which was always in her keeping, and a new shirt, partly finished, which she had intended as a present to Daniel, she burst into tears, and, shutting the drawer, threw herself in agony upon the bed. She tried to pray, but she could only exclaim, amid her sobs, "Oh, Lord, remember Lewis! Dear Lord, take care o' my poor chil'n!"

At length she fell asleep. And in her dreams she thought she followed the wagon which contained her child, on and on, over plains and through forests, he all the while laughing and clapping his hands, till at length night overtook them, and the driver called out to her that she must return. And as, with a last despairing look, she began to retrace her steps, she thought her little Lewis became suddenly conscious that she was leaving him, and screamed out, "Oh, mammy, take me, take me!" She would have rushed to him and borne him off in her arms, but his purchaser caught him fiercely back, and putting his hand over his mouth to stop his cries, drove on faster through the black concealing pines. She awoke in terror, which was succeeded by joy, at finding it was only a dream. Lewis had always slept in a little trundle bed at her side, and, for the moment, forgetting what had happened, and wishing to re-assure herself, she called out, in the manner she was wont to awaken him, "Lewis! Lewis!" But the room was dark and still; and then the truth, more terrible than any dream, flashed upon her mind, and she sank down in hopeless grief upon the bed.

But the morning stays not for any sorrow, and with its coming Sally roused herself to attend to her work, for the girl whom she had hired to help her was away for a few days, and this was one of her busiest seasons. She went about her tasks mechanically, for, to her mother's heart, the incitement to labor was at an end when there was no one to be benefited but herself. Weeks went by, during which she went her daily rounds in a kind of stupor, and of which afterward she could remember nothing. Her flesh wasted away, and her step, which was once so elastic, grew slow and heavy. She would often go to the drawer and take out Isaac's Bible, and weep over it, and wish she could read its comforting words, but it was a sealed book to her, and carefully she would return it to its place. She knew many verses by heart, and these she would often repeat to herself. Among these was, "Come unto me all ye that labor and are heavy laden, and I will give you rest." Yes, she would say, "Dat's what I wants, Lord—rest; I's allers been seekin' for it, but, Lord, I can't find it." Yet in one way she did find rest. She had received into her inmost heart by a living faith, the story of Christ's sufferings and death, and she felt that, in some way, every trial she had, if borne for His sake, brought her nearer to Him and heaven. Losing his son had made her husband reckless and neglectful of his business, and more and more given to intemperate habits. This would have seemed to her a great affliction, had she not had a greater one constantly to bear. Another trial she had, too, in the jealousy of her neighbors, both blacks and whites. It was rare for a slave woman to be so well situated to show what she could do for herself as Sally was. The constant increase of her customers, and her popularity with them, her tidy house, her neat dress, and her self-relying, independent manner, called forth many envious and malicious remarks. Often, at the market, she would hear such things as this from the white people around her: "Wonder if Sally's master's always going to let her live in this way. She's getting altogether too smart for a nigger. We shan't know who's to rule by-and-by." These unkind words went to her heart, but she took no outward notice of them, thinking it wisest to keep on her quiet way. Sometimes the bitter thought would come into her mind, "Why should I lose husband and children, and be blamed and disliked for my honest efforts to earn a comfortable living?" And then she would still such repinings, and say, "It's de cross de Lord lays upon me, an' I'll bar it for His sake."

One morning, some four months after Lewis was taken from her, as she was busy in the market, some one called out to her—

"Eh, Sally, is that you!"

She turned quickly round, and saw, in the rough-looking man before her, the purchaser of Lewis.

"That boy, Lewis, that I took out in the last lot, belonged to you, did n't he?"

Eagerly she answered—"Yes, mas'r, he's de youngest of my chil'en. Mebbe ye'll tell me whar he is?"

"Wal, he's down in Claiborne, on the Alabama river. There was a gentleman there took a mighty fancy to him, and paid a big price for him, that he did. He's a smart little chap. Should n't a minded keeping him myself."

"He loved his mammy so, mas'r! Did n't he take on when it come night?"

"In course he did. Such young uns allers do. It's nat'ral, you know. He screamed and cried for two or three nights, and I said nothing, 'cause you see, I thought he'd get over it himself. But he did n't, and at last I got tired of it, you know, and I just took him and give him a sound whipping, and he was still as a mouse all the rest of the way. That's the way to manage children."

"Oh, Lord!" was all Sally could say.

"Wal, as I was going on to tell you, I come through Claiborne on my way back here after another lot; prime ones, too. some on 'em is; first rate bargains; and as I passed by the gentleman's house, there I saw Lewis, with half a dozen other young uns, playing about the yard. I stopped my horse, and called out to him, 'Lewis! Lewis!' Then he ran down the walk, and, says I, 'I'm going back to Fayetteville, where your mammy lives; what shall I tell her?' He know'd me well enough, and he thought a minute, and then, says he, 'Tell her to send me some cakes;' and I promised him I would. Ef I was in your place, too, I'd send him some clothes. He looked kind o' ragged."

"When are ye gwine back, mas'r?"

"Wal, I reckon about the first o' the week. One of my gals has run away, and I don't mean to start 'till I get her. Strange they can't take it peaceable like, and not give folks so much trouble. So you jest fix up your bundle, and leave it down to Miller's store, and, if 't aint too large, I'll take it."

"Thank'ee mas'r, thank'ee," said Sally, "p'raps ye'll have a drink o' coffee," and she handed him a smoking bowl full, which he swallowed with great satisfaction.

"La, now," said he, "that's the real article. I'm sorry you lost your boy, but then we must expect such things in this world of trial," and with this comforting reflection which the steaming coffee had inspired, he wiped his mouth with his yellow silk handkerchief, and passed on.

It was now Saturday morning, and when her duties were over, Sally hastened home, and, making a small bag of strong calico, she filled it with Lewis' favorite hard gingercakes and crackers. Then, going to the drawer which contained his clothes, she took out article after article, and folding them, laid them together, till she came to the pretty cap, over which she hesitated, saying, "I specs he'll never go to meetin'; dere's no use sendin' it; but in a moment she exclaimed, "Yes, I will. Dey shall see how well off he was when his mammy had him." So they were all tied up together in a neat parcel, and taken to the appointed place, Sally only reserving for herself, as a memento, the little torn apron he had worn the morning before he went away. When she entered the store, the speculator himself chanced to be there, and, giving him the bundle, she said, "Will you please to tell Lewis his mammy says he mus' be a good boy, an' not grieve for her?"

"Oh, you need n't trouble yourself to send that message. "S'pose he's forgot by this time that he ever had a mother." A low groan was Sally's only answer as she turned away.

Sally now began to wonder that she was left so long undisturbed by her new master, whom she knew to be extravagant and reckless. A fear sometimes entered her heart that she might be suddenly seized and sold as her children had been, but she tried to be hopeful, and to banish it for the sake of her husband. Alas! her fears were not unfounded.

One morning, about a year after Lewis was sold, she had been to market as usual, and had purchased a barrel of flour, which was standing outside of the door. Two gentlemen entered, and the girl who helped her being busy, and supposing they wished to buy cakes, called to her in the best room to come and wait on them. She went out quickly, but as they were looking about without speaking, she took a chair and sat down, waiting for their orders. At length one of them got up and began to walk around. An undefined terror seized her. Was she sold? Suddenly he stopped before her, and looking her full in the face, said—

" Sally, *your 're mine.*"

" Oh, Lord! whar do ye live?"

"I live down in Alabama."

"Oh, then," said Sally, "I could n't cry. 'Peared like I was stunned, an' the life died out o' me. I did jes' as he told me without sayin' a word. 'You must come along now,' said he, 'and I'll see about your things afterward.' So he took hold o' my arm an' led me to the door, an' I walked along with him like I was in a dream, till we got to de slave-pen, an' den he pushed me in, an' locked me up wid de rest."

CHAPTER X.

THE SLAVE-PEN.

It is not dying that I fear;
  Lord! it were sweet to die,
And safe from all that wounds me here,
  Within thine arms to lie.

But O! 'tis living that I dread,
  When friends and love are gone,
And not a star is overhead
  To shine my night upon.

And yet, if thou would'st have me live,
  My Master and my Friend,
Unmurmuring days to Thee I'll give,
  For thou the cross dost send.

As the door closed upon her purchaser, and the terrible reality of her fate burst upon her, Sally's unnatural calmness deserted her, and she sank to the ground in a swoon. The slave-pen was an enclosure of perhaps a hundred feet square, surrounded by a high board fence, and entered by a small gate or door. In it, some thirty men, women, and children— the men chained together, two by two—were waiting their departure to the far south-west. A dreadful scene it was. Some were cursing and swearing, and some were rending the air with their cries. There were wives torn from their husbands, and husbands from their wives, and children snatched from their parents, and parents bereft of their children. Without, many of their friends and acquaintances were gathered, talking to them through the bars, some in anger and some in grief, which could find no words for its expression. There were two speculators in company; Sally's purchaser, who attended to outside matters, and who was naturally a kind-hearted man, and another, who was wholly sordid and unfeeling and whose business it was to stay with the slaves, and to act as overseer, keeping them in order as he saw fit. He walked among them, flourishing a whip in his hand, listening to their conversation, and watching narrowly any seeming attempt to escape.

It was a bright day in June, and the country was in its summer prime. All about them were cultivated fields, and away in the distance the dark pine forests stretched to the horizon. The boughs were full of singing birds, and every breeze was odorous of roses and jessamines, but in that little spot there was anguish enough to shade the brightness of the world, and to make all the angels weep as they looked down out of the clear heaven!

In the loud talking and confusion of the place, Sally's entrance was not noticed. She had lain for some time unconscious, when the overseer observed her, and brandishing his whip about her head, giving her at the same time a slight kick with his heavy foot, he called out, in a rough voice—

"Come, wake up, old gal! Don't want no fainting fits here; all my folks must be lively."

So rudely roused, Sally made an effort to sit up and look about her, and as she did so, he turned away, and was soon occupied in the distant corner. Poor Sally, her heart sickened at the scene before her, and she bowed her head upon her hands. Now and then some fearful oath came to her ear, and anon a piteous exclamation. She thought over all her life, from her childhood to this bitterest hour; a gloomy reach, with only here and there an illumined portion, like a November's day in northern latitudes, when black clouds hurry across the sky, and sunny gleams appear only now and then between the shadows of the howling winds. Would the night never come? She longed for death, and if, in her woeful state, she could have prayed, she would have besought the Lord that it might not tarry. She was roused from her reverie by the entrance of her purchaser. Seeing her sitting motionless where he had left her, he exclaimed, " Come, Sally, there's no use in grieving—what's done can't be helped. I'll take you back to the house now to pick up your things."

At these words, all the realities of her situation came vividly to her mind. She thought of her husband and of Isaac, and of her old mother, who was now owned by a gentleman a little way out of the town, and with a " Yes, mas'r," she arose and followed him. On through the streets they passed, and by the very market where she had that morning made her purchases with so much of independence and satisfaction. What a change had a few hours wrought. Now she was weak and dizzy, and led by a man who had over her absolute control. The real reason of her sale was that her success and popularity had awakened so much envy and jealousy, that it was deemed expedient she should be removed. Alabama was then what Texas is now. Her peace and comfort were nothing compared to the safety of the cherished institution of slavery, and so they were sacrificed without one pang of remorse, as they have been thousands of times since her day. She was well known in Fayetteville, and the rumor of her sale spread rapidly through the town. As they passed on, such remarks as this fell upon her ear:

"Good enough for her."

"Yes, yes; she's held her head rather too high."

"Ah! that's the way to take down your smart niggers. Reckon she wont be quite so much of a lady down in the Alabama clearings."

But they were not all ill-natured remarks which she heard. In one group was a poor white woman with whom she had often shared her simple meal, and who was now protesting against her fate.

"I tell you it's a mean shame. There aint a better woman in Fayetteville, white or black. Did n't she help me take care of Jimmy all through the fever last fall, and bring me a cup of coffee and a bit of bread whenever he was too sick for me to go to my day's work? I say we'd any of us better be sold than Sally. Any how, I believe she's got the Lord on her side."

These kind words touched Sally's heart, and for the first time that day the tears came to her eyes. *Was* the Lord on her side? In the depths of her heart she prayed that He would not desert her in this most desperate hour. "Oh! Mas'r," she cried, when she could speak, "I's willin' to go with ye if it's de Lord's will, but I'se got a son, my oldest chile, out on de Ridgely plantation, an' a little ways from him my ole mother, an' her I haint seen dis three years—if I could only bid 'em good bye!"

"Well, Sally, if you'll be peaceable and not

make me any trouble, I'll send for 'em to come and see you to-morrow morning."

"Thank'ee, Mas'r," was her grateful reply.

When she reached her own house, how deserted did everything already look. The landlord had been there, and taken her newly-purchased barrel of flour for rent; the young girl who assisted her had fled in affright, and the rooms were in confusion. The speculator kept guard at the door, and called out to her to make haste and get ready her things. How hard it would have been to her to leave the various articles of household and personal comfort, which by hard labor she had gathered together, if her thoughts had not been engrossed by greater sorrows. Only a limited amount of baggage could be carried on the long journey, and Sally was restricted to one trunk and a bag, a bed and a tub and a pail. The three last were speedily put in readiness, and then she prepared to fill the trunk and the bag with her clothing. One thing after another was taken from the drawers and folded away, and when she came to Isaac's Bible, she placed it in the bag, that she might give it to him on the morrow. While thus employed, her husband suddenly entered the house. He was away at his work when the news of her sale reached him, and, almost beside himself, he had hurried home to see her once more. Superior to him in thought and energy, he regarded her with a kind of veneration, and was weak as a child at the thought of losing her.

"Oh, Sally, ye shan't go. I can't live without ye. I'll tell dat ar cursed speculator to"——

"Don't go on so, Lewis, I can't bar it; I specs it's de Lord dat sends him."

"Sally, ye know I's got some money dat I's been savin', an' I know where there's them that'll lend me some more. I'll buy ye of him;" and he went to the door and offered the man two hundred and fifty dollars, the price he had paid for his wife; and when this was refused, three hundred dollars was proffered, with the promise that the money should be paid to him that very evening.

"There's no use talking about it," said the speculator, "money can't alter this transaction. Sally's going to Alabama, and you may as well be quiet about it."

"Oh, Lord Jesus!" gasped Sally, as the

words reached her through the open door, "go thar with me!"

Half frantic, her husband came back, and now raving, and now embracing her, he watched her lay the last things into the trunk upon the floor. "What do ye carry yer clothes for, Sally? He'll sell 'em to get grain for his cursed horses. I would n't take any thing but what I had on my back."

At this moment the speculator called out to know if Sally was ready, and hastily fastening the trunk, and leaving it with the other things which were to be conveyed to the wagon, and taking the bag in her hand, she went out, saying to her husband, "Bar it as well 's ye ken, Lewis, an' cum an' see me in de mornin'."

Eve was not sadder at leaving Paradise than was Sally when she stepped, for the last time, over the threshold of that humble dwelling, where had passed the only bright days she had ever known. Twilight was fast fading, and the hush of a tranquil summer night was settling upon the town. Who could have thought so much of anguish was in human hearts on such an eve! Silently they walked on, Sally and her master. At the corner of one of the streets she was accosted by a colored man named White, who had always been very friendly to her. Just as he passed her he said, in a low tone, which was unheard by her companion, "I shall come up to de yard to see ye in de evenin'." When they reached the slave-pen, it was quite dark, but out by the wagons a huge fire was burning, and its ruddy glow shone even on the faces of the poor creatures within the enclosure. Most of them were sleeping, worn out with the misery of the day. Sally took the most quiet corner, and laying her bag down against the fence, had composed herself as well as she was able, when she heard some one speaking to her through the bars. It was White. He had come to tell her that the speculators, having locked the door, had gone away for a little while, and that if she would wait till they were all asleep, and the fire had burnt low, she could climb over the fence and escape. A wild hope of freedom sprung up within her, and she embraced it as eagerly as an imprisoned bird that had beat its wings hopelessly against unyielding walls, would fly to an open window which revealed the sunny sky. Carefully she took the clothes from her bag and passed them, piece by piece, through the crack to her friend without, and then, when all was quiet, and the firelight glow had faded, she tried to mount the high fence that she might let herself down upon the other side. A difficult thing it was. Two or three times she almost succeeded, and then fell frightened back upon the ground. Just as she was about to attempt it again, in a different manner, the bolt of the door was suddenly withdrawn, and she knew that the master had returned, and that all was over. So quietly she lay down, and closing her eyes as if in sleep, resigned herself to her fate.

The morning dawned bright and beautiful on the fields, and wan and wretched on that imprisoned band. The slave train was to leave before noon, and life-long leave-takings must be crowded into these brief hours. Only a favored few were permitted to enter the yard; most of the poor creatures were standing by the fence, talking through it to their friends without, strangely intermingling oaths and sobs and loving words. Here and there one was heard calling upon God, and committing a friend to His care, but most of them seemed desperate and reckless in their woe.

Sally stood, looking out between the boards, to see if, among the multitude, she could discern her mother or her child. The sun rose high in heaven, and the dew forsook the grass, but still they did not come. She began to fear they had not been sent for, when, hastening through the crowd, she saw a tall and comely boy leading an old woman by the hand, whom she knew to be her son and her mother.

Calling to them that they might know where to find her, she sat down by the largest opening in the boards, and gazed out upon them as if all of life were in her eyes. Her old mother was growing childish, and her heart was almost broken at parting from Sally, who was her only daughter and her pride. Her screams and groans were agonizing to hear, and pierced poor Sally's heart with a keener sorrow. Isaac seemed quite stunned and silenced by the blow, but deep thoughts were at work within him, and he was forming resolutions which were to influence his future life. Among the slave company was a young girl of good disposition and character, named Charlotte Rives. The grandmother knew her, and begged Sally, as she desired the blessing of the Lord, to watch over and protect her. While they stood thus talking, Sally's husband made his way to the group, with wild, sad face, that betrayed a night of pain. He gave her a small parcel, saying, "There's a new dress for ye, Sally. When ye get to Alabama, if ye think it'll do for me to come, find somebody to write to me, an' I'll surely go to ye."

"I will. Lewis, I will. I'll pray to de Lord to let ye come."

"Sally, I can't stay to see ye go. It would kill me. If ye hear any thing from little Lewis, send it to me in de letter. Farwell!"

"Oh, God o' mercy, farwell, farwell!" said Sally, as they wrung each other's hands, and parted.

There was a great commotion now about the yard; then the door was opened, and the speculators entered, and took out first the chained men, whom they arranged in marching order, and then the women and children followed. Last of all came Sally, and as soon as she was without the door, her mother and her son clasped her in their arms. White, upon some pretext, had brought her bag to her again, and now, drawing from it the precious Bible, she put it into Isaac's hand, saying—

"Read it every day, chile, an' pray to de Lord to guide ye. 'Pears like he'll take care of ye. If ye see yer brother Daniel, tell him his mother loves him, an' wants him allers to be a good boy."

"Oh, mother," said she to the old woman, "you'se been a good mother to me, an I can't half thank ye for it. Do n't take on for me. De Lord 'll bless ye, an' bring us all together, I hopes, in de Kingdom."

Around Sally stood many of her acquaintances, who had been accustomed to attend the same meeting with her, and who prized her friendship, and had come out from Fayetteville to bid her adieu. Some were weeping, some invoking God's blessing upon her, and one was improvizing, in a minor strain, a song which began—

"Sister, far'well! I bid ye adieu,
 I'm sorry to leave ye, I lub ye so well;
 But now you are going to whar I dunno;
 When ye get to yer station, pray for poor me!"

But now the train was ready, and the impatient overseer called out to Sally, "Come, hurry up there! You'll have time enough to cry on the road." One last embrace, and the mother and daughter and son tore themselves from each other's arms, casting back agonized glances as they moved away. Suddenly, the old woman broke from her grandchild's hold, and running after her daughter, untied her checked apron from her waist, and threw it toward her, asking her own in exchange, which was given. Simple pledge! yet was it as dear to them as if it had been a girdle of gems.

"Far'well, far'well, the Lord bless ye," they cried, till their voices grew faint in the distance, and then the grandmother and the boy returned to their respective masters, and Sally went forward to unknown lands.

CHAPTER XI.

THE SLAVE-GANG.

Over its bed the river rolled,
   All flecked with shining foam;
The waves were black and the waves were cold,
But, deep in their darkest, chilliest fold,
   I would I had found a home.

Oh, it had been a sweet release,
   Secure from a master's call,
There to sleep in unbroken peace,
Till the world and the worldling's power should cease,
   And the Lord be all in all!

In the slave-coffle were about twenty men, with three women — Sally, the young girl Charlotte, and an old woman named Hagar, whom the speculator had bought at a bargain, and five small children. The men were chained together, two by two, but Hagar was docile from age and habit, and Charlotte from youth and inexperience, and there was a kind of dignity about Sally which made her new master dislike to put her in irons; so that, contrary to the usual custom, all three were left unshackled. The speculators rode in a light carriage, and a large wagon, drawn by horses, contained the baggage of the company. The children took turns in riding in the wagon, and now and then the privilege was extended to one of the women. What a hopeless company it was that dragged its weary way through the pine forests to the far southwest! All had been torn from home and friends, and were going every hour further from what they held dear. Is it strange that their steps were slow, and that every gloomy and evil passion was aroused in their hearts?

Poor Sally had borne up bravely hitherto under her successive trials, and had still looked forward with something of hope to the future, but this was too much, even for her endurance; and when the last farewell was over, her heart died within her, and a darkness, which might be felt, settled down upon her soul. She thought God had forsaken her, and she dared not pray. One only desire filled her mind, and that was to escape from her master, and find her way back to her dear old home. The first day they advanced about ten miles, and encamped for the night in a little opening among the pines. A heap of light-wood was soon collected, and a blazing fire kindled. The meal and water were given to the women to mix for bread, which was baked in the ashes and then divided, with a small piece of bacon for each, among the company. But this was not the white men's fare—oh, no! They had wheaten bread and crackers, and a pot of coffee boiled for them upon the glowing coals, of which the negroes could only inhale the delicious fragrance. They ate their delicate bread and drank their coffee, seeing their captives the while devouring the coarse cake, with as much indifference and unconsciousness of injustice as you would have in sitting at a luxurious table and watching your dog picking the bones at your feet. When the meal was over, the men were chained to the trunks of trees, and to the wheels of the wagon, and the women and children lay down beneath the shelter of the tent. So closely were they watched by the overseer, that they had little opportunity to speak privately to each other, but Sally had the young girl Charlotte by her side; and whispering to her to keep awake, she waited until all was still but the heavy breathing of her companions, and then motioned to her to steal out after her into the open air. She was only ten miles from Fayetteville; she would never be so near it again, and the thought made her desperate to return. Silently they crept along, startled by every wind that stirred the pine boughs, and halted between each step to listen. They had passed the tents and the wagon, and were just striking into the forest, when they heard voices. Just at that moment, the fire caught a new faggot, and, by the blaze, they saw the two speculators sitting over the embers, closely engaged in conversation. Sally was so frightened that she stepped hastily forward, treading upon a dry branch, which broke with a crackling noise.

"Who's there?" called out the overseer, as both he and his companion rose and advanced quickly toward the wood.

"Oh, mas'r," said Sally, more dead than alive, "it's only me an' Charlotte; we's jes' gwine to de spring for some water—dat's all."

"Don't tell me none of your lies," screamed the overseer; "I know what you're after, and I know what you'll get, too!" and he shook his fist in her face.

"Hush, Jones, let her alone," said the speculator; never mind about the water to-night, Sally; go back and lie down with the rest."

AUNT SALLY. 117

"Yes, mas'r," said Sally, thankful to escape, as she slunk back with the girl to her old place in the tent.

"She deserves a hundred lashes, Leland," said the overseer, as she turned away, "and if I had my way, she'd get 'em. You know she meant to run off."

"Well, I s'pose she did, and I do n't wonder at it. I tell you, she was better off than we are, and it's mighty hard to be broken up in this way. I can't afford to lose her, but I won't have her whipped for trying to run away. Now remember."

"I should like to know how such a chicken-hearted man as you come to be in this business, any way?"

"I was brought up to it; my father was in it before me, but I'm sick of it sometimes, that's a fact." And he walked slowly and thoughtfully to his tent. Poor man! He had moments of great uneasiness, for his heart was yet tender. But interest and custom were stronger than his sense of right; so, after a little disquiet, he lay down and slept soundly in the midst of his victims.

What a night was that for Sally! In her dreams she lived over the day, and Isaac's agonized face was before her, and her mother's scream and her husband's farewell rang in her ears. Bewildered and feverish she awoke. The sun had not yet risen, but the camp was astir, that they might be on their way before the heat of noon. A breakfast, like their evening meal, and then the tents were folded, and the day's march began.

Fifteen miles a day was their average travel. In the first thirty miles out of Fayetteville, they met several country farmers going into town with their produce. Some of them Sally knew, having had dealings with them in the market. They looked wonderingly at her as they passed, while she, poor soul, as she saw them disappear on the homeward road, was almost tempted to break from the line, and follow after them, even though she should be shot down in the attempt. All other feelings were swallowed up in her one desire to escape. If their path led through the forest, she wondered if she could not steal away under its shadow, and at night she lay awake for hours, trying to think of some plan by which to fly and elude pursuit. Siberia never fell colder and more fearful upon the ear and heart of the departing exile than did Alabama upon hers. She remembered the story of the flight of the Israelites from Egypt, and she sometimes thought, perhaps, the Lord would appear for her and give her a marvelous deliverance. But day succeeded day, in monotonous travel, bearing her farther and farther from home, and affording her neither opportunity nor pretext for retracing her steps. She did not quite despair, however, but, every night, when she lay down by the camp-fire, she hoped something would happen to favor her on the morrow.

Five lingering weeks had passed, and the train had wound its toilsome way quite across the Carolinas to the Savannah River, which, swollen by recent rains, rolled its black waters, flecked with foam, downward to the sea. They halted on its banks to prepare for the crossing. The carriage and baggage-wagon were to go over a ferry at some distance above, but the expense was thought too great for the party to be conveyed in this way, and so it was decided that they should ford the stream. At this a dreadful consternation seized the slaves. Naturally timid, and from their field life unaccustomed to the water, they feared to encounter its rushing tide.

Shrieks and curses were heard among them, and the jaded limbs of many a stout man quaked in his fetters. The speculator was to go by the ferry, and was giving the overseer some directions about their place of meeting, when Sally stepped forward and said, in a trembling voice,

"Please, mas'r, what river is dis?"

"It's the Savannah river, Sally."

"Oh, mas'r! have we done got past Car'lina?"

"Yes, Sally, you've seen the last of it."

"Is dat ar Alabama?" pointing across the river.

"Oh, bless you, no. That's Georgia. We've got hundreds of miles to go yet."

Sally could not speak, for such a faintness came over her that she thought she was dying. With the word Carolina was associated all she knew of home and place, and Georgia and Alabama were as vague and indefinite as if they had been in another world. But there was no time to waste in thought. The women and children were made to go first into the stream, followed by the men, who were fastened together in a line, and ordered to assist them. At the first plunge into the water, they screamed and almost fell down in their fear, but the overseer was behind them on horseback, shouting and swearing and urging them on. Desperation was in their hearts, and no ray of hope lighted up their future. Most of them would rather have died than gone forward to the misery beyond, and tried to bury themselves beneath the water, but some were afraid of death, and struggled madly to keep above the waves; so with cries from the half-drowning women and children, and oaths and fierce wranglings among the men, at last, panting and exhausted, they reached the Georgia shore.

Sally looked back at Carolina, sleeping in the afternoon sun, and knew she never should see it more, because that fearful river could not be crossed again. "Oh, then," said she, "'peared like something burst inside of me, and I gin up altogether."

And now the most toilsome part of the journey commenced, for all hope of escape was gone, and they were exhausted by previous travel. New scenes were about them. The pine groves of the Fayetteville region had given place to the more varied forests of Georgia. A richer vegetation clothed the earth, and flowers and birds, which they had never seen before, made the woodlands gay.

But Sally went forward unconscious, like one in a dream, and old Hagar, whose husband was in Carolina, and Charlotte, who had left a loving mother, wept and bemoaned their fate at every step of the way. The children were now carried constantly in the wagon, and the speculator, finding that the women were failing, and that their feet were bruised and swollen, ordered that they should take turns in riding also; and because the wagon was overloaded, sometimes gave up the carriage to them and walked himself. The men, who had no such relief, but must plod on from day to day, began to suffer exceedingly from the chafing of their fetters, and the master determined to have them exchanged for lighter ones, at the first opportunity. Their way lay mostly through forests and thinly settled districts, but, after a few days, they reached a village where was a blacksmith's shop, erected on purpose to shoe the horses and repair the irons of the slave-gangs which passed that way. They halted in front of it, and the negroes, throwing themselves upon the grass, were taken, two by two, into the shop, and their fetters exchanged for those which were easier to wear. In the village was a minister, a true gospel preacher, whose heart was wrung by the scenes which almost daily passed before his eyes on this great thoroughfare. As he glanced from his window in the hot noon, and saw the slaves lying there looking so spent and worn, with the chains about their ankles, his whole soul was moved, and, coming out of his house, he hastily crossed the road to where the speculator was sitting under a tree, and began to expostulate with him, and to set before him the enormity of the traffic in which he was engaged.

"What you say is all true, sir," said Leland; "but I was raised in the business, and if I do n't take 'em down, somebody else will. I assure you I treat 'em well. I drive the best gangs that go into Alabama. There 's a proof of what I say, sir; their irons were too heavy for comfort, and, at considerable expense to myself, I 'm having lighter ones made for 'em."

"I see you 're a kind-hearted man, and the last one that should be in a trade like this— driving men and women in chains through the country like so many cattle. You believe they have souls, do n't you?"

"Souls? I sometimes think their souls are a great deal bigger than ours. There's that woman, Sally, leaning against the tree yonder—she's got more soul than a dozen of some white women I know."

"And yet you can buy and sell them as if they were blocks of wood! I tell you, you are committing a fearful crime. God's word is against you, and the judgment day will be against you, when you stand there with them to give an account of your lives."

"Bless me, sir, no minister ever talked so to me before. I had a good many such thoughts myself, last year, after having a great fuss at the sale of one of my gangs, so I went to my minister in Alabama and asked him what he thought about it? 'O,' said he, 'these are unavoidable evils, and the world is full of them every where. There's no doubt that slavery's a divine institution, and if you do the best you can, you need n't give yourself any trouble about the matter.' I was quieted for the time, but ever since I bought Sally, I've been thinking the same things again; and I believe you're right."

"Then why not give up this cursed business, and do what you can to atone for your past life?"

"Well, to tell you the truth, sir, I'm poor, and if I do n't make well on this lot, I shall surely fail and lose every thing I 've got in the world. The fact is, I never could bear to buy and sell as most traders do, and so I never make much money any way. But I promise you, sir, if I can pay my debts when these are sold, and I 'll try to get them all good places, I never 'll buy another man, woman, or child as long as I live, for, as you say, it 's a cursed business."

The new irons being all adjusted, the line of march was again taken up. The speculator showed his sincerity by proceeding with more care, and paying greater attention to the food and rest of his company. Sally's distress of mind had so affected her health that she was obliged to give up walking altogether. She grew thin, her appetite failed, and her master feared she would not live till they reached their destination.

"Come, Sally," he would say to her, "cheer up. I 'm going to keep you myself. I 've no idea of selling you. By-and-by, perhaps, I'll take you to see Lewis at Clairborne."

At this she would smile faintly, and say, "Thank'ee, mas'r," and then relapse into her old indifference. At length they entered Alabama, and when she heard where they were, she burst into tears, and sobbed so violently that they thought she would die. Her master begged her to compose herself, but her grief would have its way. She refused to be comforted, and every few hours would moan and weep afresh, until they reached the house of the speculator, where the slaves were to be kept till he could dispose of them to his liking.

CHAPTER XII.
ALMOST DESPAIR.

Hear me, Lord! in mercy hear me,
  All my earthly joy is gone;
Not a star remains to cheer me
  Through the night that's coming on.

Thou! the meek, the tender-hearted,
  Gentle Jesus! pity me;
I from all I love have parted,
  Lord! I can not part from Thee!

The home of the speculator was on the Alabama river, about two hundred miles above Mobile. He had inherited the place from his father. It had a neglected look, and the house was going to decay, yet it was more attractive than most of the residences in that vicinity. There were ample grounds about it; and live oak and magnolia trees, rising here and there in stately proportions, atoned for the dilapidated appearance of the mansion. Leland was naturally a man of generous impulse, and fine sensibility, but he had been reared to his business by his father, who was utterly devoid of principle, and his whole life had been a contest between **habit** and interest, and his interior sense of right. His convictions of wrong-doing were just weak enough to prevent him from abandoning his trade, and just strong enough to keep him from making it profitable. So he went on from year to year buying and selling, but always growing poorer. His wife was a meek, gentle woman, who had no thought aside from her husband's opinion, and his only child was a bright, sweet-tempered girl of twelve years —her mother's oracle and her father's pride. If any one wanted a favor of Leland, it was the safest way to approach him through "Miss Bessie."

The sun was just setting on a sultry August evening, as the master, with his weary company, reached his own domain. Leaving the negroes in charge of the overseer, he rode hastily up the carriage way, and was greeted at the door with joyous acclamations by his daughter, and timid delight by his wife. The negro quarters were in the rear of the house, and in a few minutes Jones appeared, leading their new occupants thither.

"How is it, Mary," said Leland, as they passed by, "do you want any help in the house?"

"Why, yes, George," said his wife, "we really need a cook. It seems like I've had nothing but trouble with Sue since you went away."

"Well, then, there's just the woman for you. I bought her in Fayetteville; she kept a cake shop there, but she's sick, Mary, she's sick and miserable,—and you'd better take her right into the house and attend to her. Her master would sell her because every body said she was doing too well for a nigger. I declare, I never felt so bad in my life as I have for her, and if I can, I mean to keep her and use her well."

"O father!" said Bessie, who stood by, "may I run and tell her she's to come to the house, and not to be sold any more?"

"Yes, Bessie; cheer her up, if you can."

With light foot the little girl ran to the cabin appropriated to the women, and looking in, saw Sally lying on the rude bed, the picture of despair.

"Don't feel bad, Aunty," said she, as she put her little white hand in Sally's; "my father says you shall live with us in the house, and nobody shall carry you away."

Sally was too wretched and hopeless to

speak. She wished she might be left alone to die. She was like one who has gone through the agonies of dissolution in drowning, and to whom any attempt at restoration is painful. But the caressing hand and the kind words went to her heart in spite of herself, and she wept.

A few days of rest and kind nursing quite improved Sally's bodily health; but her greatest trouble was at heart. She thought she was abandoned of God, and that He had never loved her, or He would not have sent her such trials. There was no one to speak to her of Jesus, or to remind her that "whom the Lord loveth, He chasteneth," and so she went on, bearing this grievous burden in silence and alone. As soon as she was able, the cooking was given into her charge, and Charlotte was taken to the kitchen to assist her. Her new master's affairs were in a desperate condition. He had gone on his last trading expedition, determined, if possible, to retrieve his fortunes; but the incidents of the journey, the purchase of Sally, and the reproof of the minister, had aroused his slumbering conscience, and called forth all that was generous in his nature; and he was resolved not to part with his negroes except to their advantage as well as his own. So, instead of selling them at public auction, he sent privately to those whom he thought likely to buy and to prove good masters, and invited them to come and inspect the "lot" on his own premises. And now he realized, as he had never done before, the horrors of that institution which he had been helping to maintain. It began to be a fearful thing to him to have the destiny of human beings in his hands. The levity with which the subject was treated was painful to him, and the oaths and coarse jokes of the buyers grated upon his ears. And thus it came to pass, that although every day was increasing his financial difficulties, weeks ran into months, and only five men and two children out of the company were sold.

Sally's position was one of comparative comfort. Her master and mistress treated her with uniform kindness and respect; and sweet Bessie always had a smile for "Aunty," as she called her. The burden had not gone from her heart, but she had grown calm; and with her keen eye she looked around and calculated the chances of her future. She had seen more than one family's pecuniary ruin, and the disaster it occasioned, and she foresaw that this would be her new master's fate, so she took her present place much as a traveler across a burning desert would take a little oasis which he knew he must shortly leave for the pathless sand. She remembered her husband's promise to come to her if she would send for him, and watched narrowly to know if it were best. She saw that slavery there was, in some respects, a different thing from what even her experience had made it in Carolina. The ties of affection and mutual dependence which at home often bound master and slaves together, seemed there no where to exist, but to give place to a forced and cheerless servitude; above all, she noticed that free negroes were always spoken of and treated with contempt. So, bitter as was the alternative, she resolved to send word to her husband to remain in Fayetteville, where he was known, and where he could at least earn a comfortable and independent living. It was the close of a bright day in winter. Sally's work was done, and she was sitting before the kitchen fire, as she always sat now when not employed, in a kind of dream or stupor, hopeless, but uncomplaining. Suddenly the door opened, and Bessie entered with a beaming face.

Oh, Aunty! I've got something to tell you. There's been a trader from Mobile here to see father, to-day, and there was one of your nice pound-cakes on the dinner table; and he said to mamma, 'Why, where did you get such a cook, Mrs. Leland?" Then father told him about you, and when he had done, the man said you was just such a cook as he wanted to take down to Mobile, and that he'd give six hundred dollars for you. But my father said he would n't sell you, for he meant to have your bones laid on the same plantation with his; and I was so glad, Aunty, I ran out to tell you. What were you thinking about when I came in here?"

"Bless you, chile, you's very good to me. I was thinkin' 'bout my husband 'way back in Car'lina. I promised to send him word 'bout comin' down here, but 'pears like dis ain't no place for him. I's bid far'well to him an' all de chil'n, an' now 'pears like dey'd better leave me 'lone. If I could only get a letter writ to him!"

"Why, Aunty, I can write you a letter. I've written three all alone; two to my teacher, Miss Martin, she's gone to Mississippi, now, and one to my grand'ma in Tennessee. I'll go right and ask my father for some paper and his pen."

In a few minutes she returned, and, sitting down, wrote, with great care, a few lines, to Sally's dictation, directing the note to "Lewis Beggs, Fayetteville, North Carolina."

"There, now! Isn't that nice? I'll ask my father to take it to the postoffice the next time he goes over there. Don't you want me to write another to your little boy down in Claiborne?"

"Oh, Miss Bessie, I dunno whar he is. He was a peart little thing! Is Claiborne a great ways off?"

"I don't know. It's somewhere by Mobile, aint it? When my father goes down there again, I'll ask him to take you and me, and then we can find out his master and see him. If I was only a grown up woman, I'd send for your husband and all your children, and you should live in my house and have good times."

"De Lord bless ye, honey! Dere aint no more good times for me nowhar!" and Sally relapsed into her melancholy silence, while

Bessie, sad and uncertain what to do, stole out of the kitchen.

A few days after this, Sally was called to the sitting-room by her master. "There, Sally," said he, "Here's one of your old Fayetteville neighbors."

Sally looked up and saw before her Mr. Wayne, a gentleman who had often purchased cakes and coffee at her stall, but had been some months absent from Fayetteville, and had not heard of her sale.

"Why, Sally!" he exclaimed, "I'm astonished to see you down here. Where's your husband?"

"Oh, mas'r Wayne, it does my heart good to see ye! He's back in Car'lina. 'Pears like dat's de best place for him. I jes' sent him a letter to stay whar he is."

"That's right. Upon my word," turning to Leland, "this is too bad. There wasn't a working woman in Fayetteville doing as well as she was. If I could afford it, I'd take her back again. Sally, do you want to send any word home?"

Thank'ee, mas'r Wayne. Will ye please to tell Lewis, dat 'taint because I don't love him dat I sent him de letter, but 'cause I knows he's better off whar he is; an' if ye see Isaac an' Daniel, tell 'em their mother never forgets em, never. Oh, mas'r Wayne, dere's one thing more," and the tears ran down her sunken cheeks, "'pears like I's lost de Lord in my troubles. Will ye go to de meetin' sometime Sunday afternoon, an' ask my ole friends to pray for me? I's parted with my home an' my husband, an' my chil'en, *but I mus' hold on to de Lord!*"

Shaking her hand, and promising faithfully to deliver her messages, Mr. Wayne set out for Fayetteville. One morning, when he had accomplished about half the journey, as he was riding leisurely along through the forest, he saw approaching him, on foot, a negro, with a bundle slung over his shoulder. As he came nearer, he was surprised to see that it was Sally's husband.

"Why, Beggs," he exclaimed, "is that you? I saw Sally, down in Alabama, and she told me she had sent you a letter not to come there, because she knew you was better off where you were. I tell you the black folks don't fare as well down south as they do in our quarters; and as for the free negroes they hate 'em. I'm sorry for you—there are not many such women as Sally, but my advice to you is, to turn round and go home, and be contented."

Poor Lewis! Almost heart-broken after Sally's departure, he had resolved to go in search of her, come what would, and had gone thus far on the toilsome journey when this intelligence reached him. Despairingly, he retraced his steps, and after many weeks reached Fayetteville, thin and feeble. He had never possessed much energy of character, and now, having no motive for sobriety and industry, he became a confirmed drunkard, and in a short time died miserably, and was buried in a pauper's grave. It was years afterward before Sally heard of his melancholy fate.

CHAPTER XIII.

SOLD AGAIN—GLEAMS OF LIGHT.

The wind is blowing o'er the woods,
   The wind of March that longs for flowers,
And waking in the solitudes
   Sweet buds to gladden April hours.
And every blossom has its bird
   To hover o'er it all day long,
With loving whispers never heard,
   Except by flower in birdling's song.

O! that there were some gentle breeze,
   Across my wintry heart to stray,
And waken on its leafless trees
   Sweet buds of hope and coming May.
And that there were some bird of love,
   Within the boughs to sit and sing,
And singing, bear my soul above,
   Where summer joys eternal spring!

It was February. Trouble had thickened round Leland till it became certain that if the slaves were not disposed of within a limited time, they would be taken for debt by the sheriff, and sold at public auction. So deeply was he involved, that it was impossible for him to retain one for himself, and he determined, first of all, to provide the best home in his power for Sally. He knew an enterprising man in Dallas county, by the name of Cone, who had purchased new lands, and was about clearing them and bringing them under cultivation, and whom he thought would be likely to need more help. So he sent a messenger to tell him about her, and ask him to come over and see her for himself, which he promised to do. True to his word, the next day, about noon, he rode up to the house. He was a man of good sense and intelligence, and of a kind heart, but violent and unreasonable when roused to anger. Dismounting from his horse, Leland met him and took him aside for conversation.

"My wife wants a seamstress, Leland," said he; "does Sally understand sewing?"

"I can tell you this, sir. When I went to her house in Fayetteville, I saw a nice silk dress, upon which she was working, lying on the table, and I was told that she was in the habit of making dresses, and doing all kinds of work for people, when she had leisure. I assure you she's a treasure, and it's mighty hard for me to give her up. I wouldn't if I wasn't obliged to. But come into the house and judge for yourself."

So saying, he led the way into the parlor and asked his wife to send for Sally, upon some pretext, that Mr. Cone might see her. One of the young negroes was dispatched for Sally, who soon appeared. Her mistress detained her for several minutes, giving her directions about her work. It was an unusual thing; and, looking up, she saw Mrs. Leland's embarrassment, and Mr. Cone's eager gaze, and at once the truth flashed upon her mind.

"Oh, mas'r!" she exclaimed in a voice of agony, "Is I sold? Ye told me I should live an' die with ye."

"Sally, God knows my heart, I meant you should; but I've lost every thing I own in the world, and if I do n't sell you, the sheriff will."

"Has it come to dat, mas'r? Well, de Lord's will be done!"

She turned away, but in a moment came back again with streaming eyes. "Oh, mas'r! I promised my ole mother dat I'd look after Charlotte, like she was one o' my own chil'en. 'Pears like I could bar it better if ye'd sell her with me."

"Yes, Cone," said Leland, "she was the girl you saw by the kitchen, when we came in.

She's young and likely, and if you'll take her, you shall have her at a bargain, for Sally's sake."

After a little conversation, Mr. Cone agreed to purchase them both, and it was arranged that he should send a man for them the next morning.

It was evening, and Sally sat, as usual, by the kitchen fire, thinking of the change which awaited her, and wondering what dreadful sin she had committed, that the Lord sent her such afflictions. She was like a plant rudely torn from its native earth, and set in strange soil, where it has hardly begun to send forth a few nourishing roots below, and to expand a few leaf-buds above, ere it is removed to a new parterre. She longed for little Bessie's sympathy, but she had gone to her grandmother's, in Tennessee. Charlotte was with her, but she was too young and inexperienced to anticipate the future with much anxiety. She wished she could pray, as she once had done, but her trust and peace of mind were gone. The embers had grown dim, and she rose to lie down to sleep for the last time in 'hat familiar room, when the door swung open, and, looking up, she saw her master enter, pale and dejected.

"Sally," said he, "you do n't feel worse about this than I do. God forgive me for ever taking you away from Carolina."

"Oh! mas'r, 't want you, 't was de Lord dat did it, an' I must be willin' to bar whatever He sends."

"Will you forgive me, Sally, for bringing you to so much trouble?"

"I'se nothin' to forgive, mas'r, you'se been very good to me. Do n't be grievin' about it, it's de Lord's will."

"Good night, Sally;" and he extended his hand. "Good night, you 've taught me more than all the ministers."

"God bless you, mas'r! good night."

Early the next morning Sally and Charlotte were on their way to their new home. They rode in a sort of lumber-wagon, which carried also their baggage. A few miles through the forest, and they came in sight of Mr. Cone's plantation. He had begun here as a poor man, but was year by year adding lands and servants to his estate. He still dwelt in a log-house, with the simplest furniture and conveniences, while his negroes were lodged in ruder cabins around him. His family consisted of his wife and four sons. Mrs. Cone was a woman of great energy of character, but ignorant and narrow-minded. She had seen little of society, and her wardrobe at this time was less valuable than Sally's, but she was ambitious of wealth and position, and envious of any one who surpassed her. She received the new-comers with a kind of coldness and severity, which made Sally feel that she would find in her the exacting mistress, rather than the sympathizing friend. Sally had never been more utterly wretched than when she lay down that night. A dreadful home-sickness, which she had not felt with the Lelands, weighed upon her heart. Spring was coming on. The leaf-buds were swelling, the woods were full of singing birds, and the winds were soft and balmy; but as she looked out in the moonlight upon the log-cabins, and the newly-cleared fields, and the broad forests beyond them, she sighed for the comely streets of Fayetteville, and was only oppressed by the untamed loveliness of Alabama.

She had been purchased for a seamstress, and the next morning early her mistress brought her a shirt to make; but she had

had so much physical and mental suffering since her old sewing days in Carolina, that she had quite lost her former skill. Fearful of reproof, she tried to fit the pieces together, but her hands trembled, and she was so weak and bewildered that she gave up in despair. Her mistress was watching her, and after a few minutes she saw her go to the door and beckon to her husband, who was standing without.

"Just come in here, Mr. Cone," said she, "Leland has cheated you. You bought Sally for a seamstress, and she can't even make a shirt."

"Oh! missus," said Sally, "'pears like I'se forgot all I knew. Dere was n't no woman o' my color could make shirts, an' pantaloons, an' dresses, better dan I, but 'pears like I'se lost my senses."

"It's doubtful if you ever had any," said Mrs. Cone, in an angry voice.

"Come, come, wife," said her husband, "perhaps Sally 'll do better after a while. There's other work enough; the garden wants hoeing and weeding—let her come out doors."

The shirt was laid aside, and Sally, glad to

escape from her mistress' eye, followed her master to the garden. Mr. Cone was preparing to build a frame house, and stumps were to be torn up, and brushwood was to be cleared away, and the ground to be leveled about the place. At all this Sally worked for the next three months, gradually gaining strength of body in the open air, but with the same sickness and despair at heart. Perhaps it was well for her that she had daily tasks to perform, so that her thoughts in working hours were necessarily occupied, but when night came, the memory of her griefs came with it. "Oh," said she, "I allers cried myself to sleep in dem days, an' dreamed all night 'bout de ole home an' de chil'en."

Mrs. Cone's cook was "Aunt Eve," an old woman who had had quite a fame in the kitchen in her younger days, and in consequence had grown very vain and tenacious of her position. She was now getting old and incompetent. Her mistress was much dissatisfied, and hardly a meal passed without complaints on her part, and resolves to make a change. One day, when some articles of food came on to the table wholly spoiled, and Mrs. Cone was questioning, as usual, what she should do, her husband said, "Why do n't you try Sally? she 's used to cooking."

"I never thought of it. I 've had no patience with her since she spoiled that shirt. She looks so solemn, and makes herself so smart in her calico dress Sundays, that I do n't take to her much."

"Well, you 'd better try her. Eve's rules are good enough, and she can show her how."

So Sally was placed in the kitchen to do the cooking according to Eve's directions. The old woman regarded it as an infringement upon her rights, and revenged herself by treating Sally in the most capricious and provoking manner. Sometimes she would refuse to tell her what she asked — sometimes she would give her wrong measures, and so it came to pass that Sally's cooking was even less satisfactory than Eve's. "Dis made missis angry," said Sally, "an' she 'd come in de kitchen an' scold me, an' crack me over de head, an' den Eve would be glad, an' would n't tell me nothin', an' 'peared like I did worse all de time. Oh, how I cried every night, an' wished I could die 'fore de next mornin'. I thought then sure de Lord had cast me off. I did n't take no pains to look nice, like I used to, nor to have my room neat. I did n't care for nothin'. One night when I sot a crying, Eliza Freeman—she married masr's nephew—she come to my cabin, an' says she, "Sally, I'm going to give you some pieces of calico to make you a bedspread, and I advise you to rouse yourself up, and try to be cheerful. *Lay down North Carolina and take up Alabama;* if you do n't, you 'll have a poor miserable time of it, any way." Well, arter she went out, I pondered on it, an' I thought p'raps I was to blame to grieve so, and p'raps de Lord had n't forsook me, more'n I'd forsook de Lord, an' I made up my mind, with His help, to try an' bar de cross, an' begin new from dat hour to serve Him. So I got up an' made de bed, and clar'd up de room, an' den I knelt down an' prayed to de Lord to be with me, an' never leave me any more. An' 'peared like He heard me, an' come down an' stood by me, an' said, 'Sally, I will.' An' den I felt happy for de first time since I left my ole home.

"The next mornin' missis sent for me, an' says she, 'Sally, how is it you do n't make things to suit me any better?' An' says I, 'I dunno, missis. I tries hard enough to do jes' like Eve tells me.'

"'Well, how did you use to do in Carolina?'

"'Why, I had my own measures, an' followed my own ways.'

"'Well,' says she, 'I want you to let Eve alone, and follow your own ways now.'

"I thought this was a great privilege, for de ole lady was mighty contrary. De next mornin' while I was gettin' de breakfast, Aunt Eve come in, an' begun to order me about, an' says I, 'Missis said I was to lay down your rules, an' pick up mine.' Then she was mad, an' went and told missis I'd sarsed her, and missis called me, an' says she, 'Sally, what did you say to Aunt Eve?' An' says I, 'Missis, I told her you said I was to lay down her rules, an' pick up mine.' 'Well,' says she, 'I just called you so Eve might know you are not to follow her ways any longer.' So I got breakfast, an' it suited, an' den I got dinner, an' dat suited, and when mas'r come home, missis told him Sally had took new rules, and now she thought she could please her. So things went on pretty well."

CHAPTER XIV.

THE LASH—FLIGHT AND RETURN.

As she lay, all faint, on the swampy moss,
  She heard the hound's deep bay,
And the loud halloo and the answering shout,
  Waver and die away.

She had no fear of the snake below,
  Nor the poisonous vine o'erhead,
But she shrank from her master's angry eyes,
  And her mistress' words of dread.

And so she lay on the swampy moss,
  All through the summer day,
And heard the bay and the loud halloo
  Waver, and die away.

OLD Aunt Eve was full of vexation to see Sally promoted and herself set aside as useless, where once she had been supreme. All her life had been spent on an isolated plantation; she had had no religious influences to soften her heart; the only instruction she had ever received had been in relation to her cooking, and her naturally violent temper had grown harsher and sourer with advancing age. She envied and hated her new rival, and longed for some opportunity of revenge. She had hardly clothes enough to make herself decent, and Sally, in kindness, gave her several articles from her own store. She had heard the story of Sally's checked apron, her mother's parting gift, and one day, seeing it drying upon the line, she secretly pulled it down, and not daring to wear it herself, secreted it, for a time, and then gave it away to one of her acquaintances. Sally was deeply grieved at its loss, but it was not till long afterward that she knew who had stolen it.

In the neighborhood where the Cones lived, religious services were held only once a month, and then in a small church, about four miles from the plantation. On one of these fortunate Sabbaths, when Sally had lived about a year with her new master, her mistress called her to her room and told her she was going to church, and expected to bring some friends home to dinner with her; and wished her, therefore, to prepare every thing in the best possible manner. Pleased with her mistress' apparent confidence in her ability, Sally went to the kitchen, and having put all her cooking arrangements in the right train, she returned to the house, the new one which had been recently completed, and, going into the dining-room, began to set the table as she had seen it done in North Carolina. Mrs. Cone was very desirous to attain to that style of living which characterized the best families in the vicinity. When she moved into her house she had purchased many new articles of furniture—among them a complete dinner-set of blue ware. This was the first day it had been used, and Sally, who had a natural taste and skill for such things, arranged it all to the best advantage. As she was putting the finishing touches to the table, Aunt Eve, who had been watching her from behind the door, thrust her head into the room, and with a malignant scowl, exclaimed, "Laws, now! s'pose you think dat's mighty nice. S'pose you think we never seed nothin' afore. Folks knows as much here as dey does in Car'lina, any day."

"I was only tryin' to please missis," said Sally, as Eve went out, slamming the door behind her.

And "missis" was pleased. Her guests complimented the dinner, and for the first time she spoke approvingly to Sally. Eve was listening in the hall, and her mistress' words of praise rankled in her heart. How should she revenge herself? She thought a moment, and then stealing slily up stairs to Mrs. Cone's room, she took a piece of chintz calico which was lying there, and pushing it far out of sight behind the bureau, crept softly down again, and looked to see if she could find her mistress alone; but she had gone back to her company and was occupied with them until late in the evening. Eve did not abandon her cruel purpose, however, but early Monday morning she went to her mistress, and told her that the day before, while she was away at church, she saw Sally go to her room and take the chintz calico and carry it off with her. Mrs. Cone was angry in a moment. All her old prejudices against Sally revived. Without considering that Eve might have told an untruth, she ascertained that the calico had really disappeared, and then, in a violent passion, despatched a messenger for Sally and for her husband. Mr. Cone was as much enraged as his wife, when he heard what had happened, and, in spite of Sally's protestations of innocence, he took her into an old out-building, and tying her to a horseblock, told her he should whip her till she confessed where she had hid it.

"Den," said Sally, "if he gin me five lashes, he gin me five hundred, till I told him if he 'd

stop whippin' me, I 'd get de calico, though I did n't know for de life o' me whar 't was. So I ran over to his mother's, she lived in a little house near by, an' asked her what I should do. Sez she, Sally, I dunno what in the world's the matter with him. I believe Polly (dat was de name of mas'r's wife) has hid it herself.' But I knew I darsn't say no sich thing, so I run for de swamp. Dey missed me, and started out wid de dogs, but dey went up de road an' I went down, an' so dey didn't see me."

Poor soul! Just as she had begun to hope for more peaceful days, this new affliction came upon her. But she had resolved, come what would, that she would never doubt or distrust her God again, and now, as she plunged into the darkest recesses of the swamp, with her back all bleeding from its wounds, she poured out her whole soul to Him in earnest prayer for comfort and direction.

It was yet early morning. The trees were dripping like rain with dews of the night. The magnolia, the dogwood, and the wild jessamine, the honeysuckle, and a thousand other flowers, made the air heavy with fragrance; and strange-looking poisonous vines, with brilliant orange flowers, clambered from tree to tree, and almost wove the branches together. Sally sought the most secluded spot, and, sitting down, leaned for support

against the trunk of a tree. In the distance
she heard the deep baying of the dogs and
the occasional call of her pursuers, but as
they were going in an opposite direction, the
sounds at length died away, and only the
songs of birds and the rustle of leaves awoke
the silence. She was in such an agony of
pain that she could not think clearly, and so
she lay in a kind of stupor, while the hot
hours of noon went by. The dimness of
twilight was setting upon the swamp when
she roused herself and began to reflect upon
her condition. She could not hope to remain
long concealed, and even if she could, she had
no means of sustaining life; she was conscious of her innocence, and she had faith
that God would protect her, and so she resolved to find her way back to her master.
But she was quite bewildered. She knew not
which way to take to reach the open country.
Just then she heard the tinkling of a bell, and
looking up, she saw a horse a little distance
from her. The bell was suspended from his
neck, and he had evidently strayed away
from pasture. The thought struck her that
by following him she might find her way to
the road and so she commenced driving him,

but taking care to let him go in the direction he chose. A little distance, and the firm ground was gained, and then a path which led to the highway. She was so stiff and sore from her wounds that it was with difficulty she could move, and when she came to a little brook, she stooped down and bathed her back in the cool water, and wetting her handkerchief that she wore, pinned it again over her shoulders. The day had been intensely warm, and now the thunder began to mutter in the sky, and the big drops of rain began to fall, and soon there was a drenching shower. But the horse went on and Sally followed, till at length they came to a small house by the road side. Hearing the bell, the occupant, a white man, came out and secured the horse, and seeing Sally, asked her where she came from. She dared not tell him the truth, and so said that mas'r Cone had sent for her to come and do some sewing at his house, but that in trying to go there she had lost her way. "Why," said the man, "you're ten miles out of your course, but you can stay in the barn here to-night, and to-morrow morning I'll put you in the right road." So she went into the barn, thankful for any shelter, but her back was so bruised and mangled that she could not lie down. All that weary night she sat up, tormented by pain, and waiting with fearful anticipation until the dawn of day.

True to his word, in the morning the man called her, and, taking her into an open wagon, drove for several miles in an easterly direction, and then, stopping where two roads met, he helped her to dismount, saying, "This is Mr. Johnson's plantation, and the next is Mr. Cones's. Follow your right-hand road, and three miles will take you there." Sally thanked him from her heart, and he rode away.

Among the slaves on Mr. Johnson's plantation, was an old man called "Uncle Joe," who was famous with the negroes for his kindness and tact when any one of them was in trouble. Sally had often heard of him, and to his cabin, which stood a little apart from the rest, she now directed her steps. He was at home, for on account of his age he was excused from much active labor. Sally told him her story without reserve, and asked him what she had best do. He gave her some food, of which she was greatly in need, and advised her to remain in his cabin for the day, and at night to make her way toward home. His wife dressed her wounds, and did all that sympathy could do to inspire her with courage. They were godly people—this aged slave couple; they had seen much of sorrow, but through the Lord they had triumphed over all. Sally took sweet counsel with them of the things of heaven, and before they parted they prayed together, and then sung one of those hymns, full of repetition, so meaningless when written, but so eloquent to the sensitive negro heart when sung:

"Oh, when I'm in trouble here,
Lord, when I'm in trouble here,
   Give me Jesus! Give me Jesus!
You who will may have dis world—
   Give me Jesus!

"Oh, when I've an hour of peace,
Lord, when I've an hour of peace,
   Give me Jesus! Give me Jesus!
He's the only friend I want,
   Give me Jesus!

"Oh, when I'm a-going to die,
Lord, when I'm a-going to die,
   Give me Jesus! Give me Jesus!
Over Jordan glad to go,
   Give me Jesus!"

Sally bid her kind friends farewell at evening, but as she walked along, she could not make up her mind to go directly home. The church was about half a mile away, and to it she bent her steps. When she reached it it was dark and silent, but darkness and silence had no terrors for her, and she went in and sat down to rest herself, and to try to sleep, feeling that for the time she was secure from danger. The night passed, and the morning came. She half resolved to go boldly home, and then her fear overcame her resolution, and so, fluctuating between determinations and misgivings, the day wore away. About noon, some wagoners encamped near the church, and, making a fire, cooked their dinner there. Faint with hunger, Sally watched them, and after nightfall, she stole out to see if they had left any remnants of their meal. In the ashes she found several half roasted potatoes, which she eagerly ate, and, feeling strengthened, she decided, with the first morning light to go straight to her master.

With the earliest ray in the east she commenced her walk, and the sun had not yet risen when she came in sight of the dwelling.

Concealing herself behind a tree in the yard, till some friendly servant should appear, by whom she could send word to her master, of her arrival, she prayed God to help her, and to "prepare the way" before her. In a few minutes, she saw Martin, the waiter, going toward the house with some kindling wood in his hands. He was a good-natured fellow, and she at once came forward and spoke to him. How thankful was she when he told her their mistress had found the calico behind the bureau the day after she ran away!

Her fear was gone and she stepped boldly into the house with Martin, who went to his master's door and told him Sally had come. Mr. Cone came quickly out, and Sally, brave in her innocence, stood there, erect as she might with her wounded shoulders, to receive him. All trace of anger had gone from his face; he was even embarrassed as he advanced to meet her.

"I am glad to see you again, Sally. Where have you been all this time?"

Sally was afraid to say she had received any assistance from a slave, because she knew they would be severely punished if their kindness was known, so, praying God to forgive the falsehood, she replied,

"I stayed in de church, mas'r, an' some wagoners give me something to eat."

Just then Mrs. Cone came into the room. She knew the fault had been hers in accusing Sally so hastily, but she was too proud and willful to acknowledge it, and so did not speak.

"Wife," said Mr. Cone, "I'm mighty sorry for this, and I tell you I'll sell Sally before I'll ever whip her again."

So she was dismissed to her cabin without a word.

CHAPTER XV.

THE TYRANNICAL MISTRESS—A SLAVE'S SABBATH.

Grant me strength, oh Lord, I pray,
For the burdens of the day;
Let me leave to-morrow's sighs,
Till to-morrow's sun shall rise.

How, I know not, yet I feel,
Though Thou dost Thy face conceal,
Tenderest eyes are on me bent,
From the azure firmament,

And will watch me all the way,
Till the dawn of heaven's own day;
Till my life shall be begun,
Where they need nor moon nor sun!

For three weeks Sally was unable to lie down in bed, on account of the severe blows she had received at her whipping, and she was excused by her mistress from cooking, but at the end of that time she was thought well enough to resume her usual duties. All the cooking for the house was to be done by her, and, in addition to this, she had her daily task of sewing on the shirts and trowsers for the slaves. This she often had to do at night, by the light of the fire, when her day's house work was over. Sally's was no well-ordered northern kitchen, stocked with conveniences. It was a small cabin of one apartment, in the rear of her master's house. At one end was the fireplace, but about as much smoke settled down in the room as went up the chimney. She had very few cooking utensils, and was obliged to use the same kettle and the same spoon for half a dozen different purposes. Hurrying from morning till night, broiling over the fire or busy at her needle, her weeks went by. To make her labor yet harder, she had to cut her own fuel and to carry it from the woods to the house, often doing it at night and to bring all the water she used from a spring some distance away.

Mr. Cone was prospering in the world, and his wife spared no pains to improve in their style of living. She began to require more elaborately prepared meals, and poor Sally was taxed to the utmost to accomplish all which was expected of her. Every day, in her little kitchen, she made delicious pies and cakes for "the house," but she was never allowed to taste them—if she did, she was sure to be whipped for it by her mistress. Mrs. Cone was not above using the whip with her own hands when anything offended her, and as Sally had been legally made over to her at the time of her purchase, she felt that she had a peculiar right to control her as she pleased. Sometimes she would make the women whip each other, but they soon learned to make seemingly heavy blows very light. Sally had always had tea and coffee and sugar in Fayetteville, and now it was very hard for her to be deprived of them when her labor was so severe. Sometimes, when the breakfast was unusually nice, her mistress would send her a cup of coffee, but this was not often; and so she sat up at night to knit and to do little odd jobs of sewing, that she might earn money enough to purchase these luxuries for herself. Mrs. Cone had had for years a habit of occasionally drinking brandy. As she grew older, her desire for it increased. Unknown to her husband, she kept it always in her closet, and although she never became intoxicated, she often drank so much as to be very irritable and unreasonable. When at length her husband discovered it, he was greatly grieved. He was a member of the church and of the temperance society, but he could not control his wife, for she would send slyly for brandy by the servants, who dared not disobey missis' orders; and so, when he saw that she was under its influence, he would shut himself up in his room, and sometimes ride over to his plantation and stay for days together. So Sally was left to the entire control of a woman always cold-hearted and exacting, and at times tyrannical and cruel. Shut out from sympathy and friends, with nothing before her but thankless, monotonous toil, to what did she turn for comfort?—for the heart lives by loving, and must find rest somewhere. It was to God that she looked. One by one her earthly supports had been taken away, and she had learned to live by faith in the Invisible. Day by day, in her simple way, she was living out the truth of those texts which higher and more cultivated natures find it so difficult to receive and to practice, "Pray without ceasing," and "Sufficient unto the day is the evil thereof."

"Every mornin'," said she, "I asked de Lord to go with me through de day—to help me make de pies an' cakes, an' to show me how to please missis, an' den I felt contented, whether I was whipped or not."

Had Sally forgotten the past, that she was thus quiet in the present? Oh, no! She never laid her weary head upon her pillow without thinking of her mother, and her husband, and her children, and praying God to bless them wherever they were, and to unite them to her in the "New Jerusalem." In this world she never thought again to see them.

Sally grieved most for the pleasant Fayetteville Sundays, when, with her family about her, she had gone to church and heard the Bible read, and the singing, and the sermon. Sunday on an Alabama plantation was a very different thing. All the servants who worked at a distance came home on that day to see their wives and families. Tired out with the labor of the week, it was, notwithstanding, the only time they had in which to do any thing for themselves. They were required to keep their clothes clean, and this was the only day on which they could wash them. Then those who had a patch of ground given them to cultivate, wanted this time to work upon it. Some took the opportunity to go fishing, keeping part of the fish they caught as a treat for themselves, and selling the rest to their mistress to obtain a little money for buying flour or molasses. But most of them were too tired to work, and would throw themselves down anywhere upon the ground, and sleep through the day like so many dogs. Bred to nothing but physical exercise—having only their animal nature cultivated, and constantly overtasked, what else could be expected? When they finished their work early enough on Saturday evenings, they sometimes had a prayer-meeting in a grove at a little distance from the house. Sally could not attend this, nor the meeting on Sunday morning, "But gen'ally," said she, " I could get about half an hour to go down to de afternoon meetin', when de folks was at dinner. We did n't have any preacher dere who knew how to read, our deacon could n't read a word, but 'peared like he allers knew what to say. I know he talked right well, for I used to notice when I went to de church, an' 'peared like he talked just as de minister did. Den, after he 'd exhorted, I 'd have to go away, so they 'd sing some far'well hymns, and den I 'd go back to de house. Dis yer was one of de hymns I loved to sing:

"'I have a place in Paradise
To praise the Lord in glory;

O, sister! will you meet me there
To praise the Lord in glory?
By the grace of God I'll meet you there,
To praise the Lord in glory.

"'The blessed hour, it soon will come,
To praise the Lord in glory;
Oh, brother! will you meet me there
To praise the Lord in glory?
By the grace of God I'll meet you there
To praise the Lord in glory.'"

Sally had joined the Baptist church soon after she was purchased by Mr. Cone, but she was never allowed to attend the services except on Sacrament Sundays, when her master insisted that this privilege should be granted her. The church was several miles away, and she had to make such haste in going and coming, on account of the dinner, that these were to her the most tiresome days of the year.

Sabbath afternoon was the favorite time for training dogs to hunt negroes. When not in use, the dogs were always kept chained, and no colored person was allowed to speak to them, or to feed them, under the penalty of a severe whipping. At training times, the dogs were let loose, and put on the track of a little negro boy, who was made to climb a tree. When they could trace him unerringly to his place of concealment, they were considered trained.

Such sights as this greeted Sally on the Sabbath. Every evening in the week there were family prayers at the house, which were free to all the servants. Sally longed to listen to the Bible, and she always went, excepting when her mistress had treated her so harshly that she thought to hear her read would do her more harm than good. Thus, with very little change, year after year passed away. Mr. Cone's sons were growing up about him, one of them, Stanley, into an idle, dissolute young man. Sally had heard nothing from her children, but she continued to show to Charlotte Rives, now married to the coachman, the kindness and care of a mother.

"I had heaps 'o trouble, den," said Sally, "I did n't 'spect to get rid of it; I did n't look forward to nothin ; but *I jes' picked up de cross an' put it in my bosom*, for de sake of de dear Lord who carried it for me so long ago!"

CHAPTER XVI.

NEWS FROM A LONG-LOST SON.

Thank God! he lives, my precious boy!
The world can give no purer joy!
He breathes the air that's breathed by me—
The sun shines on him—he is free!
But let him roam where'er he will,
He is my boy, my darling still;
And the same God who hears my prayer,
Will hear him, watch him everywhere—
The Slave, the Free—my faith is dim,
But heaven's as near to me as him;
And every day, though foul or fair,
We're drawing nearer, nearer there!

Sally had now lived twenty years with the Cones. She had been so accustomed to her life there, that her earlier days seemed to her vague and shadowy as a dream. In all this time she had heard nothing from her mother or her children; she only knew that her husband, Lewis Beggs, was dead. She thought of them, she prayed for them, but it was almost as for those long since passed out of life. It was rare in that region for a slave to escape in any way from bondage. She never looked forward to this. Death was to her the gate of freedom and the beginning of joy.

During all these years she had been but two or three times absent from the plantation, and then by special permission. Her mistress had often been solicited by visitors at the house, to let her go and teach their servants her ways of cooking and arranging tables, but she always refused upon some pretext or other. About this time there was to be a merry-making at a wedding among the slaves on an adjoining plantation, and Sally was invited to be present. Her mistress chanced to be in a pleasant mood, and so gave her leave to go. Delighted with the thought of a holiday, Sally made haste to finish her work, and a little before dark on the evening of the appointed day, arrayed in a clean gown and turban, and with her "pass" in her hand, she set out with the other servants on her way to "Mas'r Blake's." When they reached there they found quite a company assembled, the younger people dancing to the music of a violin. Sally was glad to see all her acquaintances, but she had no heart for such merriment, so she retired to the farther corner of the room. She soon noticed, sitting apart from the rest, a forlorn looking man, in torn, rough clothes, to whom no one seemed to pay any attention. Her kind heart was moved with compassion, and she took up her chair and sat down beside him, and began to talk to him.

"Good evenin'! 'Pears like you're a stranger here. Whar d'ye come from?"

"I come from de Car'lina rice fields.'

"Laws now! Dat's whar I was raised. Mebbe ye knows some o' my folks. Did ye ever hear o' de Williamses?"

"Why, sartain I did. Dere's one o' 'em, Mary Ann Williams, dat lives in Mobile. I knows her right well."

"Laws! Ye don't say! Why she's my own cousin, but I haint seen her dis thirty year. What she doin' dere, an' how come you to know her?"

"Wal, ye see she's got a good master, an' she hires her time an' takes in sewing an' makes well on 't. I goes on de river, an' I heern tell of her, how she come from de rice-fields, an' nat'ally when I goes to Mobile, I goes to see her, an' we talks 'bout de ole places."

"To be sure! to be sure! When 'll ye be gwine back?"

"I 'specs de boat 'll go to-morrow mornin'. We run smash 'gin anoder boat dis arternoon, an' we's jes' waitin' till dey can 'pair her. Dat's de way I come to be here."

"Would ye take a little bundle for me to Mary Ann?"

"Sartain I will, an' I 'll go 'long wid ye now an' get it."

The interest of the party was all over to Sally, so getting up quietly she went out.

Among Mr. Cone's servants was a boy about fifteen years of age, called Nero, who had always manifested for Sally the affection of a son. He was remarkably sprightly and intelligent, and, secretly, getting one idea here, and another there, he had taught himself to read with a good degree of ease, and to write a tolerably fair hand. Sally's plan was to get him to write a letter for her, so she beckoned to him, and, taking him aside, told him what she wanted. He was delighted to do it for her, and the three were soon on their way to Mr. Cone's. Arrived at her cabin, Sally kindled a little blaze on the hearth, while Nero produced from his store a pen and ink, and a small piece of paper, and wrote the letter to her dictation. It suddenly occurred to her that Mary Ann might have forgotten her, or would not feel sure that she had written the letter. What proof could she give her?

When her mother came to bid her good-by at the time she left Fayetteville, she had given Sally a small plaid shawl, which their old mistress Williams, the deaf and dumb lady, was accustomed to throw over her shoulders when she first rose in the morning, and which she had presented to Sally's mother. It was a singular-looking shawl, and she knew Mary Ann would remember it, and that it would serve to establish the identity of both. So she put it into a little parcel with the letter, and asked the boatman to give it to her cousin, and to return the shawl again to her, which he promised to do.

When he had gone, Sally lay down and tried to sleep, but a thousand thoughts were in her mind. Hopes and desires which had slumbered for twenty years waked to life. Her children, her friends, her early home, came back in memory, and the old home-sickness and longing filled her heart. She began to wonder if she could not go to Mobile and see her cousin with her own eyes, and resolved that she would speak to her mistress about it on the morrow, and so thinking, she fell asleep.

When morning came, she thought it wisest to delay speaking to her mistress until she had actually heard from her cousin, and so she waited anxiously till the "Magnolia" should return, and the boatman bring her an answer to her letter; and every day she prayed that, if it was God's will, she might not be disappointed. Two weeks passed, during which she heard nothing, and she had almost given up hope; but one night, about nine o'clock, as she sat half asleep by the fire, she was roused by a tapping at her door, and, opening it, there stood Daniel, the boatman, with a bundle and a letter from Mary Ann. Neither of them could read it, so Sally stole softly out for Nero. He was as pleased as she was to find that an answer had really been received. It was in Mary Ann's own unpracticed hand, and it was a long time before Nero could decipher it. It was a cordial letter, expressing great joy that Sally was alive, and, too wonderful for belief, telling her that her son Isaac had some years before been in Mobile with his master; that he had sought out his cousin Mary Ann, and inquired earnestly of her for his mother; and that since then he had written her that he had purchased his freedom and was a Methodist minister at the North!

Sally was quite overcome by this sudden and joyful news. Again and again she would have the letter read to her. She would hardly have believed its words had not the shawl been returned with it, with the message that she remembered the way their old mistress used to pin it on, and had not her cousin sent her also a new calico dress. It was like that older surprise when they told Jacob, saying,

"Joseph is yet alive, and he is governor over all the land of Egypt. And Jacob's heart fainted, for he believed them not. And they told him all the words of Joseph which he had said unto them; and when he saw the wagons which Joseph had sent to carry him, the spirit of Jacob, their father, revived, and he said, 'It is enough; Joseph, my son, is yet alive; I will go and see him before I die!'"

When Daniel and Nero had left the cabin, and Sally was alone, she burst into tears of joy, and falling on her knees, thanked God for His great mercy, and consecrated herself anew to Him. That her son was living was happiness enough—that he was a free man and a minister, quite outran her conceptions of good.

There was nothing objectionable in her cousin's letter, so the next morning she carried it to her mistress, and while she read it, she said to her in a trembling tone,

"Please missis, if you or Miss Eliza traveled on de boat as de ladies do, an' would take me with you down to Mobile, I should so like to see Mary Ann!"

"No, Sally, I never travel."

"Well, 'pears like, if you 'd let me go sometime?"

"No, Sally, you can just give up thinking any thing more about it—it's altogether too far from home."

Sally took the letter, upon which no comment was made, and put it safely by; but sleeping or waking, the thought of it was ever present with her. "A few weeks after this," to use her own words, "I was a-getting supper, an' mas'r called me, an' I was scared, for I did n't know what was de matter. I tried to think if I had done anything, but thinks I, 'you 've got to go,' for mas'r was one of de men, if he told you he 'd whip you, he would.

Well, I went in an' stood by his side, an' he had a paper in his hand, an' says he,

"Sally, whar'd you live?"

"Near Fayetteville, on Haymount Hill," says I.

"Who were your neighbors?"

So I told him.

"What was your husband's name, and what was he sold for?"

So I told him that, an' then says he,

"Sally, here's a letter from your son Isaac, sure!"

Well, I could hardly believe it; but says he,

"Sally, he wants to buy you. Now you've paid for yourself many times over, and if you can get your mistress to give you up, you know you belong to her, I'm willing."

So I went right and spoke to mistress about it, an' says she,

"Sally, it's not my mind any way," an' then she'd have nothing more said about it, only she was dreadful cross to me. Isaac kept writin' to mas'r, an' wanted me to tell him 'bout things dat happened when he was a boy, an' when I did, he wrote back dat he know'd 't was his mother. Missis whipped me more 'n ever, 'cause she thought I'd feel kinder independent 'bout Isaac's wantin' to buy me. I was allers thinkin' 'bout it, but I did n't dare let missis know, an' when she spoke 'bout Isaac, I 'd say,

"Poor fellow! he wants to see his mother, but I guess he never will."

Mas'r was all de time tryin' to coax missis to give me up. One day we had company to dinner, an' missis was very happy with her chil'n round her, an' mas'r asked her 'fore all de gentlemen, if she did n't pity Sally when she wanted to see her son. I knew she 'd be mad, so I got out of the room as quick as I could, I was waitin' on de table, and prayed de Lord to soften her heart. Sometimes I gin up altogether. It was a consolation to me to think about de grave, an' I thought if my son did n't get me, I 'd be there to rise with 'em in the mornin'.

CHAPTER XVII.

THE LIGHT OF HOPE AT LAST.

Out of the storm the rainbow comes;
From midnight gloom the stars;
The moon that silvers thousand homes,
Climbs first o'er cloudy bars.

And every morn's the child of night;
There is no other way;
O may this life, so void of light,
Give birth to heaven's own day!

A year, full of suspense and anxiety to Sally, passed away. Isaac wrote frequent letters to the Cones, begging them to name the price at which they would sell his mother. Mr. Cone would gladly have parted with her, but her mistress, to whom she belonged, was unwilling to lose so valuable a servant. Ever since she came there, Sally had lived in the little smoky kitchen, but now, in order to make her situation as pleasant as possible, her master built for her, in the yard, a small frame house with a brick chimney, and placed in its one large room several convenient articles of furniture. She had still all the family cooking to do, but she had better facilities for her work, and a good bed to sleep upon when it was over. She dared not speak to her mistress about her freedom, lest it should make her more determined not to release her. She felt that prayer was her only resource, and through the busy day and the quiet night, her thoughts went up to God in yearning supplication that He would soften her mistress' heart. As Mrs. Cone had grown older, she had become somewhat milder in character. She had been for years a member of the church; and now, when Isaac's letters came, entreating her to sell his mother, she began to feel that perhaps it was her christian duty to consent. So she finally said her husband might write to him that she would part with Sally for four hundred dollars. She did not believe he could ever raise so large a sum, but she had quieted her conscience by naming a price.

Isaac was now the pastor of a struggling church in Detroit, with a family dependent upon his exertions for their daily bread. It was long before he was able to do much toward collecting the money, but in this interval he wrote many letters of affectionate cheer to his mother. Sally never despaired She had taken up her cross and carried it whithersoever her Lord had led her, and now she had faith to believe He would grant her this joyful crown.

At length, Isaac raised the whole sum, and transmitted it, as had been narrated, to her master.

"'Fore de money come," said Sally, "I never said nothin' 'bout it. I was as still as a dumb creetur, but when I knew mas'r had really got it, den I felt independent."

In the evening of the day upon which it was received, Sally was summoned to her mistress' room. "Hope deferred maketh the heart sick." She had become so nervous from the delay, that the least thing agitated her. Trembling she went in, and sat down in a chair which her master gave her.

"Well, Sally," said he, "you're your own mistress now. There's a letter from Isaac, with a check for four hundred dollars."

"Oh, mas'r! de Lord be praised!"

"Why, Sally," broke in Mrs. Cone, "are you so glad to leave your old home?"

"Oh! missis, I's sorry to leave you an' mas'r—you's been good to me, an' 'pears like I shall feel kind o' strange anywheres else; but den, I's goin' to see one o' my chil'en! To think what de Lord has brought me to! I thought I should carry de cross clar down to de river, an' now He's given me de crown 'fore I gets to Jordan!"

"Well, Sally," said Mr. Cone, "I didn't think 't would come to this; but I'm glad for your sake. Isaac must be a fine fellow. You're to go on the boat next week, in charge of a gentleman, all the way to New York, and there you'll meet your son. He has sent you five dollars to buy a dress, or anything you may need for the journey; and he handed her the money.

Five dollars! Sally hadn't had half as much money in her possession since her old cake-selling days in Fayetteville.

"Laws now, de dear boy," she exclaimed, (he was still to her the boy whom she had left twenty-five years before,) I 'spects he needs it himself; an' him sendin' all dis money to buy me. I shall take it to get something for him an' de chil'en;" and bidding her master and mistress good night, she went to her house.

The news of her freedom was already noised

abroad among the slaves, and she found quite a company awaiting her arrival. Twenty-five kind and blameless years had won for her the respect and affection of all her fellow-servants, and as she entered, they crowded around her; and in their simple way, some with tears and ejaculations, and some with jokes and laughter, they congratulated her upon her good fortune.

"Oh, my friends," said Sally, "dis is more dan I ever 'pected. I hope de Lord 'll make me humble. I thought I should live and die with ye; but 'pears like dere's something else for me to do. I mus' go whar de Master calls, but I shall never forget ye—never. We'll have a good meetin' together 'fore I goes away, but now ye mus' leave me alone with de Lord."

Quietly they went out, and Sally's overcharged heart poured itself forth in thanksgiving to Him who had led her through such a wondrous gate of joy. All the bitter sorrows of sixty years faded away, and her grateful thoughts dwelt only upon her unexpected mercies. She forgot the unkind treatment of her mistress, and the trials from the servants when she first came to live with the

Cones; she loved them all, and remembered them in her prayers.

Mrs. Cone was much affected by the humility with which Sally received the news of her freedom. She was sorry to part with one whose services were so valuable to her, for Sally, though sixty years old, was still strong and active; and, more than this, she began to be troubled at the thought that she had not done her christian duty by her. These feelings disposed her to be very lenient now, so she allowed her to call on the neighboring ladies to bid them good-by, and to sell her bed to one of them, (the feather-bed she had brought from Fayetteville,) and to keep the money for her own use. Sally was a favorite with the neighbors, and they gave her various articles of clothing as parting presents. She obtained permission also to send to town, and there, forgetful of self, she expended her five dollars in purchasing a stout pair of shoes for Isaac, and various gifts for his children.

It was the night before she was to leave Alabama. Her "free papers" were in her possession, her worldly goods were all packed in an old trunk her mistress had given her, and she sat in the center of her kitchen, surrounded by Mr. Cone's servants and a few from a neighboring plantation, who had come to bid her farewell. They were all sorry to part with her, and longed to know more of that freedom to which she was going. For a moment a gloom seemed to overspread the circle, when one old woman exclaimed,

"Well, Sally, arter all, de Lord's jes' as near to us here as He'll be to you dere."

"Yes, yes!" said Sally, "dat's de greates' comfort; we never can lose de Lord. If we love Him, He'll allers stay by."

Then she spoke to each one separately, and shook them by the hand, and exhorted them to meet her in heaven. It was with sobs and tears that they sang this favorite farewell hymn:

"Farewell, brother—farewell, sister—
'T is the Lord that's calling me,
Never more shall I behold ye,
Till we all his glory see
In the new Jerusalem.
Blessed Jesus!
In the new Jerusalem.

"I have come through many perils,
Foes without and foes within,
And the fight will ne'er be ended,
Till I'm free from every sin

In the new Jerusalem.
Blessed Jesus!
In the new Jerusalem.

"Then when all our toils are ended,
　Gathered on that shining floor,
We will praise our glorious Leader,
　Brother, Friend, for evermore,
　　In the new Jerusalem.
　　Blessed Jesus!
　　In the new Jerusalem.

"Farewell, brother—farewell, sister—
　'T is the Lord that 's calling me,
Never more shall I behold ye,
　Till we all His glory see
　　In the new Jerusalem.
　　Blessed Jesus!
　　In the new Jerusalem."

Silently they went out, and Sally was left alone. As they crossed the yard, Nero suddenly came up to one of the women and said, in a hurried whisper,

"Oh, Aunt Sue! has Sally gone?"

"No, Nero! but she's a-gwine to-morrow mornin'. We's jes' been biddin' her good-by."

"Dat's good; I was afeard I should n't see her agin. I stole away from de plantation, cause I know'd dey would n't let me come if I asked em."

"Well, Nero! I knows she'll be glad to see ye. De Lord knows we's all sorry 'nuff to have her go, but we could n't 'spect her to stay when her son's paid de money for her. Oh, dear! dere was my Sam dat dey whipped to death 'cause he would try to run away. If he'd a lived, he'd a been jes' like Isaac. Oh dear, dear!"—and the poor creature went to her cabin, and Nero tapped softly at Sally's door.

"Bless de Lord! Nero," said she, as she opened it, "I thought I should go away without seein' ye."

"Oh, Sally! 'pears like I can't have ye go noways. Dey sold me away from my mother, an' now dere's nobody dat cares for me but you."

"Do n't take on so, Nero. I's sorry to leave ye; but de Lord's in Alabama jes' as much as whar I'm agoin'. You's been very good to me, an' I never shall forget ye."

"Sally, I do n't want to live here, I want to be *free*. When I think about it, 'pears like I can't stay here another day. Sometimes I almost conclude to run away, but dere ain't much chance for dat."

"Oh, Nero, ye mus' n't talk so. P'r'aps de Lord 'll prepar de way one o' dese days."

"Why Sally, He's let you live here sixty years."

"Well, chile, I's tried to bar de cross, an' now He's givin' me de crown, de crown o' joy. Dat's what we mus' all do, an' den, if he sees best, He'll give us de reward, even in dis world; but if He do n't, *we's sure of it in de kingdom.*

"I 'll remember ye, an' when I gets to New York, I 'll tell de people 'bout ye, and mebbe dey'll some on 'em buy ye. Keep up a good heart, an' the Lord be with ye!"

It was late, and afraid to stay longer, the poor boy tore himself away.*

The night passed and the morning came. Sally was up with the sun, and assisted for the last time in preparing the family breakfast. When it was over, her mistress came into her house with a shawl over her shoul-

---

* The boy, Nero, now nearly twenty years of age, is still living on the Alabama plantation, and doubtless yearning for freedom. According to Sally's account of him, he must possess unusual ability and excellence of character.

ders, and, accosting her very pleasantly, asked her to go out and take a walk with her.

"Yes, missis," said Sally, and together they went out, her mistress leading the way, till they came to the fowl-yard, where she sat down upon a fallen board, and motioned Sally to sit beside her.

Sally's meek and consistent course had had a deep effect upon Mrs. Cone. She was softened and humbled by it, and now that she was about to leave her, she desired to make all the reparation in her power for the long years of indifference and severity.

"Sally," said she, "I want you to pray with me before you go away, and I want to pray with you. We shall never see each other again."

"No, missis," said Sally, "not in dis world, but I shall allers pray for you an' mas'r, an' all de chil'en."

"Sally, if I've ever done wrong by you, I hope you'll forgive me."

Sally was wholly overcome by these words of her mistress. She forgot all she had suffered. Her heart was full of love, and the tears ran down her cheeks as she exclaimed,

"Oh, missis! do n't talk so. You an' mas'r's

been kind to me. De blessed Jesus has to forgive us all. I'll ask him to have mercy 'pon us;" and kneeling down, she besought the Lord to bless her mistress and all those she was leaving. Mrs. Cone followed, and really subdued by the influence of the hour, she prayed for Sally as she had, perhaps, never prayed for herself.

Such a prayer as dat was!" said Sally, "'peared like de blessings she asked for me dere followed me all de way."

Together they went to the house, where the wagon was in waiting to convey Sally to the river, that she might be ready for the boat which was to take her to Mobile. Every thing was in readiness, and throwing her old cloak over her shoulders, for it was now December, she stepped into the wagon.

"Good-by, Sally," said her master, as he shook her hand.

"Good-by, mas'r; far'well, far'well, an' de Lord bless ye an' missis, an' all de rest—I loves ye all, an' hopes to meet ye above."

The house servants were gathered about the door, and there was not one among all the company, master, mistress, or slave, who did not say, "God bless ye," as she drove away.

A last look at her little cabin, "the house," and the fields around, and then feeling that all old ties were sundered, and that God alone was leading her, she bade adieu to the plantation for ever.

CHAPTER XVIII.

HOPE REALIZED.

And in her arms she held at last
    The loved and lost of years,
And clasped him to her bosom fast,
    While, 'mid her falling tears,
She murmured softly, fondly o'er
    The name that in his youth he bore.

And days of toil 'neath southern skies,
    And nights of bitter pain,
Were recompensed as from her eyes,
    Ran down that blessed rain,—
The while she murmured fondly o'er
    The name that in his youth he bore.

On a bright morning in January, 1857, one of the employees of Adams' Express Company entered the store, on Broadway, of the merchant who assisted Isaac in transmitting the money for his mother, and going up to the desk, presented a "bill of lading" to the clerk, and asked if it was "all right?" The clerk handed it to the merchant, who examined it for a moment, and then with an "All right, sir," gave it back again, ordering the amount to be paid. The expressman waited for the money, and then went out to his wagon before the door, where, amid bales and boxes, was one precious article of freight, consigned to the merchant's care, nothing less than Aunt Sally from the Alabama plantation!

There she sat, like one bewildered, amid the bustle and splendor of Broadway, looking first on this side and then on that, and peering anxiously into the face of every colored man who passed, as if she would fain descry the features of her son. The man assisted her to dismount, and the merchant, whose heart as well as whose influence, had been enlisted in her redemption, led the way into the store, and gave her a seat in the farthest corner, where she was soon surrounded by a group of eager listeners. As she walked up the long aisle between the laden counters, she might have been taken for a witch of old, or a Meg Merrilies, so strange and grotesque was her appearance. Her shoes were of stout, undressed leather, such as is worn on the plantation; her gown, that hardly reached her ankles, was of linsey-woolsey; over her shoulders was thrown a long loose cloak, and round her head was wound a red and yellow Madras handkerchief, surmounted by a bonnet of erect crown and brim, probably some cast-off finery which her mistress had worn twenty years before. A most remarkable bonnet it was—one that would not have disgraced Cripp's case of "Paris Styles," or Tiff's description of "dem roosts o' bonnets dey w'ars at camp meetin's."

But Sally was all unconscious of the sensation her appearance created, and earnestly inquired for her son. She seemed much disappointed when told that he was away from the city, and might not be home for several days.

"Laws now!" she exclaimed; "I thought he'd be de firs' one I should see when I got to New York."

"Do you think you shall know him," Sally?"

"Well, 'pears like I shall; but I dunno. He was a likely lookin' boy."

The question arose as to how she should be disposed of till Isaac's arrival. She knew no one, but begged to go where she could make herself in some way useful. A gentleman in the store, Mr. L., who lived in Brooklyn, said that his wife's cook left her that morning, and that if Sally chose to assist her, she might go home and remain with him. To this she gladly consented. Meanwhile she was becoming accustomed to everything about her, and began to relate, with much ease and spirit, many of the incidents of her life.

So the day passed, and at evening she went with Mr. L. to Brooklyn. She was kindly received by the family. A small room was given her for her own while she should stay, and she was told not to feel that she must rise early in the morning, but to consult her own pleasure about what she did.

Who can describe her feelings as she lay down that night, for the first time feeling that she was a free woman in a free land? Think of it. Sixty years old, and her birthright only just attained—more than half a century of toil and pain before she could feel that she had a right to herself! "Fore dis," said she, "I allers felt dat I belonged to mas'r. My hands was mas'r's—my feet was mas'r's—

I was all mas'r's, 'cept my heart—dat was de Lord's."

Her thoughts were so full of prayer and praise that it was long before she could compose herself to sleep, and then it was but to renew in dreams the wonderful experiences through which she had passed. Awakened in the morning by the voices in the street, she thought it was her mistress calling her, and rose hastily, and commenced dressing herself, when she remembered where she was. But she did not lie down again. She went to the kitchen, and began to assist in the preparations for breakfast, uttering every few moments some exclamation of surprise at the conveniences of the house. "Laws now!" said she, " dis yer pump 's a mighty nice ting. Wonder what my ole missis 'd say to it. Why, down dere we has to tote all de water from de spring. An' dis big pile o' wood all in de shed —I allers had to go way 'cross de field for de wood, an' never had no help 'cept when Nero cut a little sometimes. Poor boy! Wish he could see dis yer. Den dat coal dat ye makes such a han'some fire with in de parlor—never seed no sich in Alabama. Laws! folks is so curis up here."

The day passed away, Sally spending most of it in the kitchen, assisting in the work of the family. "'Pears like," said she, "dis is de place for me." Two or three times Mrs. L. called her to come up and sit with her, and tell her about her life at the South. She would go, but her thoughts were evidently on her son. She inquired anxiously what time Mr. L. would return from New York, and seemed impatient for the hour to arrive. At length he came, but it was alone.

"Well, Sally," said he, "Isaac did n't come to-day; perhaps you 'll see him to-morrow. But you must n't be discouraged. It 'll take some little time for him to collect money enough to carry you back to Detroit, where he lives."

Sally tried to look cheerful, and asked him, as she had several times done before, to tell her how Isaac looked, and all that he had said about her.

Thus more than a week passed away, during which nothing was heard from Isaac. Sally grew sadder and quieter with every day, and at last really seemed ill, and took to her bed. "At first," said Mrs. L., "she was constantly singing some of her favorite hymns, whether at work or in her room, but at length the singing ceased altogether. I knew it was only from anxiety on account of her son, and I was almost as impatient for his coming as she was."

Asking Sally, afterward, about this time of suspense, she said,

"Dey was all kind to me. I tried to put my trust in de Lord, an' to think He'd bring it all out right, but at last, when I did n't hear nothin' from Isaac, I began to be afeard 't was n't him dat sent de money, an' dat de speculators had got me agin."

At length, when nearly two weeks had elapsed, Isaac returned from his visit to New Haven and the vicinity, and went straight to the Broadway store to learn the news respecting his mother. When told that she had arrived, and was actually in Brooklyn, he was quite overcome, and felt as though he could hardly wait an hour to see her.

"I will go to Brooklyn with you at three o'clock," said Mr. L.; "at three o'clock this afternoon."

Isaac had some business still to attend to, so saying he would be back at that time, he went out. But his thoughts were all with his mother, and five minutes before three, by the Trinity church clock, he entered the store. He waited till he heard the bell strike the hour, and then going up to Mr. L., who was busy with some gentlemen, he said—" It is three o'clock, sir," thus reminding him of his appointment. Mr. L. remembered the engagement he had made, and in a few minutes the two were crossing the ferry to Brooklyn. He had a hundred questions to ask as to his mother's looks and appearance and conversation, and seemed annoyed at every little delay of the boat or the cars upon which they went out to the avenue where Mr. L. resided. No wonder! He was to see her from whom he had been separated for twenty-five weary years, and whom, much of the time, he had thought dead. When they reached the house, Mr. L. took Isaac to the parlor, and gave him a seat, while he went to find Sally. She was up, and in the kitchen busily engaged in making custards for tea. He told her he wanted her to come up stairs and see some one who was waiting for her. She had almost ceased to look for Isaac, and as many of Mr. L.'s friends had called to see her from sympathy and curiosity, she supposed it was one of them, and answered,

"Yes, sir, when I gets dese yer custards in the oven."

"But, Sally, I want you to come now."

So, all unthinking, she left the dish, took off her checked apron, put on her spectacles, and followed him up stairs. Daylight was growing dim in the curtained parlor, and the gas was not yet burning. Sally stood a moment on the threshold, looking into the room, and then, all at once, the truth flashed upon her, and she sprang forward, exclaiming, "To be sure, to be sure, to be sure!" and clasped her son in her arms!

She held him tightly to her; she patted him as if he had been an infant; and when he could not speak, but only wept, she would say,

"Do n't cry, Isaac, do n't cry. I prayed to de Lord dat I might n't cry."

And he could only answer,

"Oh, mother! mother! the Lord be praised!"

Long they stood there, speaking not, but clasping each other as if they could never more be parted. By-and-by they sat down upon the sofa behind them, still holding each other's hands, and began to talk of all their past. They were left undisturbed by the family, and it was late that night when Isaac, after repeated farewells, left the house to return to New York.

As soon as he was gone, Sally went to find Mr. and Mrs. L.

"Laws now!" said she, "to think dat ar's my boy! I allers thought de Lord had somethin' for him to do, but I never 'spected he'd be such a gentleman, an' a preacher too—de Lord's been very good to me"—and bidding them good night, she went to her room. After the door was shut, they heard her singing one of her favorite hymns—

"Come, saints and sinners, hear me tell
The wonders of Immanuel,
Who saved me from a burning hell,
And brought my soul with him to dwell,
And gave me heavenly union.

Isaac had some friends among the colored people in New York, who were very desirous that he should bring his mother to stay with them, so the next day he came to Mrs. L.'s to take her away. Sally was glad to go anywhere with him, but she was sorry to leave those who had been so kind to her, and expressed again and again to them her gratitude. Mrs. L. made her a parting present of some spools of thread and some needles, with which she was much pleased. The story of her release was now noised abroad. She received many kindly attentions, and was invited to make various visits with her son. Among others, she came back to Brooklyn to spend a few days at the house of the gentleman who had been instrumental in her redemption, and it was there that the writer of this narrative first saw her. We were sitting round the blazing fire, one cold January evening, when the door-bell rung, and Sally and her son were ushered in. Perfectly black, with a face wholly negro in its characteristics, there was yet something commanding in her appearance, as with majestic form and dignified bearing she entered the room, and, speaking to the circle with ease and propriety, took a seat by the fire. There was about her that repose and self-poise to which all polite culture aspires, but which, in her was the result of the inward teachings of the Spirit, and of a life of such suffering and privation, that she had come to regard all earthly things as of little moment, and to look forward with lively hope to the fruitions of the unseen.

Her fantastic bonnet had given place to a close silk hood, and her awkward shoes, to a more elegant and comfortable pair; otherwise her dress was the same. And there, in that brightly lighted room, with the snow blowing against the panes without, she went over the story of her life, which has been reproduced, as nearly as possible in her own words, in these pages. It was wonderful, the entire absence of malice or revenge from her thoughts and words. She seemed to have forgiven all, and to love all, for the sake of her great master. Her simple piety, her ideas of self-sacrifice, and entire submission to the divine will, reminded one of Madame Guyon's highest spiritual flights.

The sabbath came, and Sally accompanied the family to Plymouth Church. While in New York, she had seen the Rev. Dr. Thompson, and was very desirous to hear him preach, but the Tabernacle was full the morning she went there, and she was unable to obtain a seat except so near the door that she could not hear the sermon. So now she was seated just beneath the platform, where every word would be distinctly audible. She was a member of the Baptist church in Alabama, and had heard no preaching there, save now and then a sermon from the ministers of that persuasion. The deep tones of the organ and the singing of the hymns by the whole congregation, were quite new to her. The sermon was one of those lucid presentations of truth for which Mr. Beecher is remarkable, satisfying the most logical intellect, and yet apparent to the simplest heart. It was evident that Sally lost not a word. Speaking of it when we reached home, " Why," said she, " I used to think all churches but de Babtis' worshiped idols, but I jes' made up my mind when I heard dat ar sermon, dat I never 'd refuse gwine into no church agin, so long as I lived in dis low ground o' sorrow. It made me feel bad 'bout mas 'r. 'Pears like it's *impossible* for mas 'r to get to heaven. He do n't cheat, nor tell lies, but den he do n't bring himself up to what de preacher said dis mornin'. Laws! if I could a' heerd dat sermon down dere, sometimes, when I felt so bad! But den 'peared like de Lord Jesus talked to me, an' dat was best of all. Poor mas'r, I hopes he'll get to heaven. I won't judge no one. We's all got to be judged one o' dese mornin's."

A moment, and she exclaimed, "What a 'markable pra'r· dat was! So humble, so beggin', so coaxin', to every poor sinner. I took partic'lar notice o' dat ar pra'r. Den de singin'—it made me think o' de hymn.

> 'We'll join de forty thousand
> Upon de golden shore!'"

Her expressions of surprise and delight at any elegances about the house were amusing.

"Why," said she, "I'se seen more at de North dan I thought was in de world. If I should go back an' tell 'em 'bout it, dey would n't believe me. Wonder what missis 'd say to dis yer carpet, an' dem picters hangin' up dere? Well, dey's all very nice, if ye do n't get yer hearts sot on 'em. Ye mus' n't do dat, 'cause I 'specs dey aint *nothin'* to what we shall see in de New Jerusalem."

There was a poor, indolent colored girl, who came occasionally to the house to beg. Sally was indignant that one who was well and able to work should live upon charity, and, feeling that she had a right to speak to one of her own race, she went out to the side-gate where the girl was in waiting, and reproved her severely for her mode of life. As for herself, she put her principles in practice, for although she was told to do only what she pleased, she chose to be busy, and asked the privilege of preparing for the table various palatable dishes which are peculiar to the South.

Before she left, the lady of the house asked her to pray with her for her children, and she said it was affecting to hear her simple, earnest words, as she besought " de great Mas'r above to bless dis dear young missis an' her chil'n."

Isaac's business was now done, his money collected, and he was anxious to take his mother to his home. She, too, was impatient to see his wife and children. They were detained some days longer than they intended by the violent snow-storms which rendered traveling difficult; but, at length, with the blessings of all who had known them, they left New York for their home in Detroit.

"Far'well, far'well," said Sally, as she went away; "de Lord bless ye all for yer kindness to me, an' bring us all together agin in de kingdom!"

CHAPTER XIX.

AT HOME IN FREEDOM AND PEACE.

My boy is mine. His children sit
At eve upon my knee;
And yonder by the cheerful fire,
His smiling wife I see.

And every face is full of love,
And every voice is kind;
I only thought in paradise
Such blissful joys to find.

O Thou! who such a heavy cross
Did'st give me strength to bear,
Grant me all grace and humbleness,
This joyful crown to wear!

THE following letter was received from Isaac, shortly after he and his mother reached Detroit:

DETROIT, Michigan, Feb. 10, 1857.

MY feelings can be better imagined than described as I left New York and turned my face homeward, accompanied by my mother. Every thing around seemed engaged to make us happy, and often joyful expressions would be heard from mother, as if she had but just begun to feel that she was a free woman. We went to Dunkirk by means of a pass given us to that point by the gentlemanly president of the Erie Railroad Company. As the cars moved from Jersey City, we each gave one hearty "Thank God!" that we had at last started for our home. We had not gone far before we became the subject of remark among the passengers. Curiosity led many to want to know something about the strangely dressed old negro woman, and they would pass and look at us inquiringly. At length, one asked mother whence she came, and where she was going, to which she said,

"I's all de way from Alabama, an' I's gwine home with my son. He's bought me."

I went into another car for a few minutes, and as I came back I found a crowd around her, each one listening with attention to what she was saying. Her eyes seemed to assist her mouth in telling her story. The news soon spread from one car to another—"A mother bought by her son!" As I heard the comments that were passed upon it, I must say that it seemed to me the proudest and happiest period of my life. At dinner time, a gentleman said to me. "Take the old

lady out to dinner, and I will pay for you both," which he did. So we went on till we reached Dunkirk, where we took the cars for Buffalo. We had a kind reception at Buffalo, and money enough was added to our little store to send us home. We reached Windsor, opposite Detroit, at half-past 11 o'clock in the evening of February 2d.

"Is dis whar we's gwine to stop?" said mother.

"Oh, no; this is only the end of the railroad."

"Den ain't I gwine no more on de cars?"

"No, we're almost home."

We now went down to the water's edge to get on board the ferryboat to cross the river.

"Are we gwine on dis yere place, Isaac?"

"Yes, mother, this is the boat."

We seated ourselves in the saloon, and were soon landed safely on the Detroit side.

"Is *dis* de place whar we's to stop?"

"Yes, this is the place."

"Thank de Lord! I's done got over travelin'. Now I wants to see de chil'en. Come, let's go;" and she started on as if she had a perfect knowledge of the way.

"Stop, mother, we're not going out yet.

It's a good ways, and I must get some kind of a carriage to take the trunks up, so we'll ride."

"I can walk, Isaac, I 's been so much trouble an' 'spense to ye dat I do n't want ye to spend another penny for me."

But a carriage was procured, and soon we were seated within and on our way through the dark and silent streets to the humble but much-loved home whence I had been absent since July, 1856.

Mother was silent till the carriage stopped at the gate. Then she said—

"Is dis de house?"

"Yes, mother."

"Den I aint got to go no whar agin."

"No, we are at home now."

I got out and gave her my hand to help her out, but she stepped down alone, and went up to the door, waiting till it should be opened. It was now twelve o'clock, and the family were all in bed, but a few hard and familiar raps on the door were sufficient to rouse them. Soon my wife opened the window and exclaimed, "I know that voice," and laughing for pure joy, she called out to the children the welcome news,

"Pa and grandma's come!"

And without stopping for many clothes, they ran down and opened the door, and received us with the heartiest expressions of love and kindness. Some one then opened the door of the front room, and mother passed into it, and I presented each one separately to her.

"Oh, mother! mother!" said my wife, "I'm so glad to see you!"

"And I too, and I too," said all the rest. Mother had heard me tell of each one and learnt their names long before, so looking around upon them, she said, "Whar's Mary?"

"Mary, my oldest child, is married and lives near by. She with her husband was at once sent for, and came, with her baby in her arms. After the most cordial greetings had been exchanged, mother seemed satisfied, and exclaimed—

"Thanks to de good Lord! He's been so good to me. See what He's done for me. Glory and honor to His name! I'd almos' gin out, but de Lord He prepar'd de way.

"Chil'n, I can't tell you how glad I is to see you all!"

An hour and a half passed away before we

really knew it, and the clock striking two, reminded us that we must let the children go back to bed, and take a luncheon ourselves. But before we separated, all joined in singing this good old hymn:

"And are we yet alive
 And see each other's face?
Glory and praise to Jesus give,
 For His redeeming grace.

"What troubles have we seen;
 What conflicts have we passed;
Fightings without and foes within,
 Since we assembled last.

"But out of all, the Lord
 Has brought us by His love;
And still He doth His help afford,
 And hide our life above."

Never in all my life did I feel just as I did then in prayer to Him who had permitted us to meet around one common altar. That night will long live in the memory of the family.

About nine o'clock the next morning, all came together again for devotions, and afterward we partook of a refreshing meal. Now mother could fully be seen, walking from one part of the house to another. She seemed perfectly happy, and would exclaim,

"How well you's fixed up! Every thing's so nice! Well, I dunno what to say, only I thank de Lord for it."

And this is the mother and this is the son, who, through such peril and labor, have escaped from bondage into freedom. The facts need no comments. They are eloquent enough of themselves. But when we remember that these are not isolated cases, but that every day there is this suffering and strife for liberty, with only now and then one fortunate enough to obtain it, they become "trumpet-tongued," and plead with us to rest not till all over the land liberty shall no longer be a *name* only, but the *right* and *blessing* of every creature.

Sally was somewhat affected by the change of climate. When a slave at Fayetteville, one of her feet was injured while she was at work in the field. It had never been very strong, and now the intense cold increased the lameness, so that for sometime she could hardly walk; but at the coming on of the warmer weather she recovered. Since she went to Detroit, she has been very desirous to obtain work as a cook by the week or the month, in order to assist her son, and also for her own peace of mind.

"Oh!" says she, "when I ain't doin' nothin' I's all de time thinkin' on 'em down dere in Alabama. Poor creeters! dey wants to be free, an' dey can't. I feel so bad for 'em! 'Pears like I mus' be busy to keep dese yer thoughts out 'o my head."

But Isaac thinks his mother has labored long enough, and is not willing she should leave his home. She seems entirely happy in his family, and does every thing in her power to contribute to the household comfort, and, in return, all try to make her life pleasant. She makes a great pet of Isaac's youngest child, a little girl, three years old, who, she thinks, resembles the little Lewis that was sold from her at Fayetteville. One day a lady called to see Sally, and, going into the house, saw only this little child.

"Where's your grandma?" said she.

"O I 'spose she's singin' 'bout her Jesus,'" was the answer. When Sally entered, the lady began to talk to her about her life, and, merely to see what reply she would make, asked her if all that was published about her in the papers was true.

"Oh!" said she, "every word on 't—every word on 't! When dey reads it to me, it makes me feel sick, it brings back de ole times so. Den I thinks so much 'bout all dem I's lef' behind. I wish dey was free. I lo so! I haint forgot 'em, none of 'em, nor poor mas'r nor missis."

"I suppose you enjoy it very much to have your time to yourself?" said the lady.

"Yes, indeed! 'pears like it's so nice to lie a-bed in de mornin jes' as long as I please. I use to think about it in Alabama, an' wonder if de time ever 'd come when I should n't have to get up soon as de day broke."

Sally never goes from home without her "free papers," lest in some way her dearly prized liberty should be endangered. She has made many visits in Detroit and the vicinity, and been received and treated with much kind attention by those who knew her history. She greatly enjoys hearing her son preach on the Sabbath, and is interested in all he is doing, and desires to help him. Uniformly cheerful, she looks at her mercies rather than her trials. She knows not whether her first husband is living or dead. She has never heard a word from her little Lewis, since the trader told her of his having been sold at Claiborne. When she last heard of her son

Daniel, he was in jail in Virginia, having escaped from a cruel master in North Carolina, and fled toward the North, and been taken up and imprisoned as a runaway slave. She prays for them all, but she looks at Isaac and is happy.

In every affliction she has trusted the Lord, and felt that He could turn her sorrows to blessings. Truly, to her the CROSS has been the WAY OF FREEDOM.

www.ingramcontent.com/pod-product-compliance
Lightning Source LLC
Chambersburg PA
CBHW031820230426
43669CB00009B/1209